*Managing Extreme
Financial Risk*

STRATEGIES AND TACTICS FOR GOING CONCERNS

KARAMJEET PAUL

ELSEVIER

Amsterdam • Boston • Heidelberg • London
New York • Oxford • Paris • San Diego
San Francisco • Singapore • Sydney • Tokyo
Academic Press is an imprint of Elsevier

Academic Press is an imprint of Elsevier
The Boulevard, Langford Lane, Kidlington, Oxford, OX5 1GB
225 Wyman Street, Waltham, MA 02451, USA

First published 2014

Notices
Knowledge and best practice in this field are constantly changing. As new research and
experience broaden our understanding, changes in research methods, professional practices,
or medical treatment may become necessary.

Practitioners and researchers must always rely on their own experience and knowledge in
evaluating and using any information, methods, compounds, or experiments described
herein. In using such information or methods they should be mindful of their own safety
and the safety of others, including parties for whom they have a professional responsibility.

To the fullest extent of the law, neither the Publisher nor the authors, contributors, or
editors, assume any liability for any injury and/or damage to persons or property as a
matter of products liability, negligence or otherwise, or from any use or operation of any
methods, products, instructions, or ideas contained in the material herein.

British Library Cataloguing in Publication Data
A catalogue record for this book is available from the British Library

Library of Congress Cataloging-in-Publication Data
A catalog record for this book is available from the Library of Congress

ISBN: 978-0-12-417221-0

For information on all Academic Press publications
visit our website at store.elsevier.com

Transferred to Digital Printing in 2013

Working together
to grow libraries in
developing countries

ELSEVIER   Book Aid International

www.elsevier.com • www.bookaid.org

Managing Extreme
FINANCIAL RISK

ELSEVIER *science &*
technology books

Companion Web Site:

http://booksite.elsevier.com/9780124172210

Managing Extreme Financial Risk
Karamjeet Paul

ACADEMIC
PRESS

Under his leadership, many of us learned the meaning of risk.

Everything involves risk because we don't know the future. It is at the center of how the financial industry drives its revenue model. Yet the word risk is used only to imply something not good.

"We read in our newspapers, and even in our business magazines, solemn words about 'risky investments' and 'risky loans,' from writers who do not seem to realize that these phrases are as redundant as talking about a one-story bungalow."[1]

Walter B. Wriston

[1] Walter B. Wriston (1986): *Risk and Other Four-Letter Words*; Harper & Row, New York.

CONTENTS

SECTION 2: Elements of Sustainaliblity Management

FOREWORD

Each of the last three decades has witnessed major financial crises: the Continental Bank and the Black Monday crises of the 1980s, the S&L crisis, the Long-Term Capital Management and the Asian Debt crises of the 1990s, and the bursting of the tech bubble and the 2008 crises of the 2000s. Extreme tail risk played a major role in contributing to the impact of every one of these financial crises.

While each crisis instigated a general sentiment for the need to do something to avoid a repeat of the experience, the crisis of 2008 has been different. Because the depth and breadth of this crisis impacted Wall Street and Main Street globally, this sentiment has been more intense and the discussion about the need to do something in a fundamental way has been longer-lasting than after previous crises.

Over the last five years, this need to "do something" has driven public-policy debates, regulatory proposals, and institutional initiatives, as well as the market's nervousness, particularly in relation to extreme tail risk at financial institutions. A lot has been done in the years since 2008 to address this need, ranging from the Dodd-Frank act to a new Basel III accord to refinement of risk models and new controls in risk management. These changes have been motivated by a desire to prevent another near-meltdown; from a systemic perspective, it is imperative for the financial industry to continue its vital role of providing liquidity and capital for the global economy. Also, from an investor perspective, it is equally critical that financial institutions avoid becoming a casualty of extreme tail risk if there were to be another financial crisis.

Almost all the changes adopted to date have been either attempts to plug a perceived hole or simple extensions of preventive controls to tighten previous limits a little more. Such changes amount to marginal improvements over how extreme tail risk was or was not addressed previously. They haven't gotten to the heart of a critical problem. What is needed instead is a fundamental change. Anything less will be no different from the reactions in the aftermath of previous crises, which—relative to the impact of these crises—amounted to something like rearranging the deck chairs.

This book suggests a fundamentally new approach to address and manage extreme tail risk at financial institutions.

Financial institutions have traditionally managed risk with a one-dimensional focus known as risk management, even though everyone knows that risk has two dimensions, like a double-edged sword. Each dimension has different implications for a financial institution. Let's frame this in a broader context.

Every for-profit enterprise has two primary objectives: (i) to capture the full financial potential of its business model (financial objective), and (ii) to always protect itself as a going concern (sustainability objective).

Today, the business of large financial institutions is centered on managing financial risk. This is done through prudent risk taking, the parameters of which are established by financial goals, such as return on equity, profit targets, and limits for earnings volatility. Such financial goals are established in the context of the financial objective of the company. Therefore, the revenue-driving dimension of risk is managed in the context of the company's financial objective.

The other primary objective (sustainability objective)—which is often not defined or quantified at all, as the survival of the firm is taken for granted—implicitly directs that the institution be run in such a way that it always maintains itself as a going concern. Survival of the firm is an imperative. This objective deals with the second dimension of risk, quite distinct from what drives the revenue engine, as detailed in this book. However, this sustainability objective is such a basic imperative that the financial objective can only be meaningful if developed and implemented in the context of ensuring that the institution will survive. If the institution is not viable, then the financial objective is irrelevant. Therefore, the financial objective can only be established within the context of the company's sustainability objective.

This establishes a clear hierarchical relationship between the two dimensions of risk, since each is driven by a distinctly different objective. The sustainability objective establishes goals for tail-risk parameters, or the sustainability-related dimension of risk. This dimension provides the context for the financial objective, which establishes goals for traditional risk-management parameters or the revenue-driving dimension of risk.

There is no choice between managing the traditional revenue-driving dimension of risk and addressing the sustainability-related dimension of risk. Both must be emphasized and managed simultaneously and distinctly. Therefore, in order to be effective and meaningful, the boards of financial institutions must establish and drive parameters of both dimensions in their hierarchical order. The critical question is, how should boards of directors establish and drive them distinctly? The CEO is the driver of the revenue-driving dimension of risk; who should be the driver of the sustainability-related dimension of risk?

Starting with a resolution of this issue and then building a mechanism to address tail risk effectively is the key to a fundamental change that will enhance the ability of institutions to survive extreme crises and lead to a stronger financial system. This book presents the case for sustainability management, and then outlines what is needed to make this change and to address the concerns that have been the focus of public-policy debates, regulatory efforts, institutional initiatives, and marketplace anxiety over the last five years.

This book is organized into three sequential sections, each building on the previous one, and it provides discussions of a number of historical events to illustrate relevant lessons. The first section, Chapters 1–5, discusses shortcomings of the traditional risk-management discipline to demonstrate the need for a new and distinct approach to tail-risk management. Chapters 6–9 comprise the second section, describing the elements of a new approach to managing extreme tail risk. The third section, Chapters 10–18, presents implementation issues and the wide-reaching impact of effective sustainability management that can lead to stronger financial institutions, greater shareholder value and a more robust financial system.

Karamjeet Paul is the managing principal of Strategic Exposure Group. With more than 35 years of operating, finance, treasury and exposure-management experience, he has unique expertise in identifying and addressing extreme exposure from tail risk. His perspective has been gleaned from extensive hands-on experience in large global organizations, startups in entrepreneurial settings, and via advisory assignments.

In the early 1980s at Citicorp, he pioneered a framework that was adopted by the firm's senior leadership to address and manage interest-rate exposure management at the institution. Over the years this framework became the foundation of interest-rate exposure/gap management at all financial institutions. He later served as CFO of a large consumer services division and the Global Investment Bank at Citicorp.

More recently, with a focus on extreme exposure from tail financial risk—combining his experience with financial and non-financial companies—he has developed another unique framework designated as "sustainability management." By defining and quantifying the extreme-exposure dimension of the risk spectrum, this framework provides the foundation for addressing critical board-level and senior management issues to ensure that the company's sustainability as a going concern is managed proactively.

He has also identified and launched new business propositions while at Citicorp and beyond. In the 1990s, he founded a consumer healthcare information service business with a unique model. He led a talented team recruited from premier companies to create the largest consumer healthcare database in the United States and the second largest consumer health publication. These assets were deployed to develop and sell innovative services to major pharmaceutical and several health-related companies.

His operating and client experience spans businesses in multiple industries, including banking and financial services, information services, publishing, direct marketing, healthcare information, online information, business process outsourcing services, manufacturing and distribution, pharmaceuticals, and consumer packaged goods.

He received an MBA from Case Western Reserve University in Cleveland OH, and graduated from Indian Institute of Technology (IIT) in Bombay India with a Bachelor of Technology degree.

As a Big Brother, Karamjeet mentored a single-parent child from the Bronx, NY for 6 years and served as an active trustee of Big Brothers Big Sisters of New York City for over 20 years.

Contact Information: KPaul@StrategicExposureGroup.com

ABOUT THE CONTRIBUTORS

This book is a collection of many concepts, perspectives, stories, and experiences gleaned from my contact with a number of people over the last 40 years. It is not possible to list all of them here to express my appreciation for the opportunity to learn from them. However, I would like to list and thank the following individuals specifically for their contribution to this book.

- Morton Glantz, an adviser to corporations, governments, investment and commercial bankers, and accounting firms, is on the adjunct faculty at Fordham University's Graduate Business School. He is widely published and has authored eight books.
- Rob Kissel is the founding principal of **Kissell Research Group.** His career includes executive-level positions at UBS as executive director of strategies and portfolio analysis and J.P. Morgan as executive director and head of quantitative trading strategies. He has authored three books and numerous research papers on trading strategies, algorithm trading, risk management and best execution.
- Craig Carpenter, following a 34-year career, retired as vice president of Continental Bank in 1994.

Some contributors have opted to remain anonymous so that they would feel more comfortable about freely sharing their perspectives and experiences. The objective of including perspectives and experiences here is not to make anyone look bad. Instead, it is to learn from their observations in relation to the theme of this book. I am very grateful to the anonymous authors for their contributions, as well as for their ongoing advice.

And, finally, I wish to thank two individuals who have contributed by listening to and commenting on my presentations, exchanging ideas, and providing guidance over the last three years as the sustainability management concept came together.

- Tom Mann retired as managing director of Société Générale in 2012 following a career that spanned Chase Bank, Equitable, and Constellation Financial Management (which he co-founded). He has since founded an institutional asset solution firm.
- Bill Filonuk was managing director at Bank of New York Mellon. He had very kindly agreed to write a chapter to provide a global perspective on extreme exposure in financial markets. Unfortunately, he passed away unexpectedly on May 25, 2013. His enthusiasm for new ideas, knowledge, energy, optimism, and willingness to help anytime is greatly missed. Thank you!

ACKNOWLEDGMENTS

There are a number of experienced professionals and senior executives who have taken interest in the development of this book and provided guidance and counseling on this project. I am grateful for their interest and help in reviewing the sustainability management concept and the book manuscript.

In addition, I would like to recognize Professor Sheffi for the guiding light provided by his book. And I wish to thank Professor Morton Glantz of Fordham University for nudging me to write this book.

And, most importantly, on a personal level, I want to thank Evan, Lindsey and Judy for their unconditional support and love, which provides inspiration for everything I do. In addition, I can't say enough to thank my lifelong partner Judy, whose constant encouragement and faith made this book possible.

INTRODUCTION

In 2006, I read a book: *The Resilient Enterprise* by Yossi Sheffi, professor and director of the Center for Transportation and Logistics (CTL) at MIT. Without using such words, he demonstrates how tail risk can impact and sometimes end up redefining companies. The book includes examples of several businesses that faced an extreme crisis. Some went down in flames; the others rose from the ashes stronger and more resilient, both operationally and strategically.

In 2007, Professor Sheffi connected me with some people at CTL. Over the course of the next 18 months, I had off-and-on discussions with some of their staff members and students; attended seminars where I met senior logistics, risk management, and operations people, primarily from non-financial companies; and even helped a couple of graduate students learn to quantify financial exposure from extreme operational risk. At first, I was puzzled and intrigued by the gap between my work of advising companies about quantifying extreme exposure from business interruption risk and the risk-management thinking of people I interacted with through CTL. Reflecting on it made me realize that most people, in managing risk, (i) do not distinguish between normal risk and tail risk, and (ii) perceive tail risk only in the abstract, and thus see tail-risk management as an extension of traditional risk management. This can create significant vulnerabilities for an institution.

Then the financial crisis of 2008 happened, and I realized that one of the significant contributing factors in the crisis was that even the financial industry, in managing risk, does not distinguish between normal risk and tail risk, and perceives tail risk in the abstract.

Once upon a time, financial institutions added primary value by intermediating liquidity between depositors/investors and borrowers. Many still do, but—with the continuing development and globalization of financial markets and relatively easier access to liquidity—more and more value from financial institutions comes from the intermediation of risk between liquidity providers and liquidity seekers. This has made the business of financial intermediaries primarily about managing risk, and over the last 20 years we have seen hundreds of millions of dollars invested in risk management. The combination of this evolution of their role and managing both normal risk and extreme tail risk under the same umbrella has critical implications for financial institutions. Actually, this is a disaster waiting to happen, as I saw in the events of 2008–2009.

Not making this distinction between normal risk and extreme tail risk is often the reason institutions lack clear, highly focused goals and governance policies for the management of tail risk. In addition to leaving them vulnerable, this makes it difficult—if not impossible—to align the objectives of regulators, who are concerned about tail risk, and the interests of financial institutions. It actually creates an ongoing conflict.

Viewed through the prism of traditional risk management, financial institutions see risk as the driver of their revenue models. Viewed through the same prism, to get a handle on extreme tail risk, makes everything institutions do seem suspect to regulators. And hence the conflict, because the traditional risk-management prism is not designed to provide a view of extreme tail risk. On the other hand, tail risk, when addressed through its own prism, can lead to a convergence of the objectives and interests of regulators and financial institutions.

In addition, viewing tail risk through the traditional risk management prism—with all the complexities that drive revenue models—can add confusion and lead to subjective conclusions at best and potential to miss critical exposure at worst.

To manage tail risk proactively and distinctly, the challenge is to define and quantify it first. This led me to focus on developing a simple, objective, and transparent measure; and the framework I call "sustainability management" was born. I believe this framework can help institutions effectively address the second of their two primary objectives: to ensure sustainability of the institution. Employing such a framework also helps align regulatory and institutional interests.

In addition to creating the concept, I found challenges in naming it "sustainability management." When I mention sustainability management, people almost always assume that I mean something related to clean energy or ecology to save our planet. This actually brings to mind so many parallels.

The dictionary defines ecology as concerned with the interrelationship between organisms and their environment. In a classic sense, sustainability is a key issue in ecology, as it refers to the resilience of organisms or natural systems to exogenous factors (generally created by humans), and is dependent on the laws of nature. Now if you change the context and make a couple of substitutions, then it is easy to think of ecology analogously for a financial institution as concerned with its relationship with the marketplace.

In this context, sustainability refers to the resilience of financial institutions to exogenous factors (created by markets) and is dependent upon the laws of economics. Preserving these parallels, but also making the natural versus market-driven distinction, I often refer to the resilience as "going-concern sustainability management."

At the very basic level, the going-concern sustainability management concept enables an institution to make wiser and more educated choices and decisions about how to deal with extreme tail risk. These sustainability management choices and decisions start at the senior-most level in financial institutions. For example:

- How do you define sustainability from the perspectives of shareholders, clients, and regulators?
- How do you establish sustainability goals and governance guidelines that maximize shareholder value, and also align them with systemic regulatory interests?

Similar to examples in Professor Sheffi's book, the financial calamities of 2008 represent an inflection point for the financial industry. And depending upon how proactively they deal with tail risk, some institutions will end up more resilient and stronger and thus more likely to survive the next financial crisis, while others may find themselves at a disadvantage. Five years after the last crisis, this redefinition is nowhere near completion yet. It has only heightened the awareness that a change must come.

While I understand and appreciate their value, I am not an algorithm, formula, and quant guy, and this book is not about algorithms and formulas. My focus tends to be on addressing questions such as the ones posed above to help formulate sound policies and develop frameworks that achieve objectives effectively. I believe that addressing such questions will also position institutions and regulators on the same page and thus alleviate systemic risk.

Going through this book, readers will realize that no algorithms and formulas are needed to start on sustainability management, although I am certain they will develop over time to optimize implementation of policies and strategies. The industry has some very smart people who can take the concepts and framework outlined here to a level of sophistication that I couldn't even imagine today. Looking back and learning from the past introduction of new concepts, I realize that the solutions suggested here could turn out to be only a crude start to a sophisticated going-concern sustainability-management discipline down the road. The financial industry will be stronger as a result.

One final thought: In as much as I have developed the concept of a measure of extreme exposure for financial institutions, I do not claim to have all the answers. As always happens with something new, the use of such a measure will initially raise more questions than it may answer; however, these questions will be more about the process to quantify the measure and how to use it than about its value.

6:15 a.m. As he walks to his trading desk, Rupert can't help feeling the conflict. Ten days ago, based upon the announcement by South Korea to curb the appreciation of the Won against the US dollar, he had committed the bank to a large, complex position in Asian and British Pound currencies. He is excited, as the position, although within his allotted limit, is the largest bet in his seven-year career at the bank. He feels comfortable holding it until next Tuesday or Wednesday. And so far so good, but the thought of leaving his desk with such a large open position for about four hours during the prime hours of the Pound trading later in the day is making him somewhat uncomfortable. Anything can happen!

At the same time, he is looking forward to seeing Ian, who was his 9th floor roommate at Hughes-Parry Hall while attending the University College London ten years ago. It has been four years since they last had a few pints together at Ian's bachelor party at Packies in Kenmare, Ireland.

Ian is in London today for barely 11 hours, on very short notice, for a client meeting in the morning. He can't stay overnight as his wife is expecting their first child any day now. So they settled on an old tradition (from their UCL days) of a Chicken Tikka Masala lunch at Motijheel restaurant on Marchmont Street. This will be followed by a few pints of lager at Mabels Tavern down the street from their old residence hall on Cartwright Gardens, before Ian takes the Piccadilly line to Heathrow for an early evening BA flight back to Dublin.

8:30 a.m. Global financial markets are operating without signs of anything extraordinary. Rupert chuckles and thinks to himself probably riding on the wrong side of the road, as he sees that a big story from the G-8 Summit is about President George W. Bush colliding with a British police officer during a bike ride. The officer had to be hospitalized.

9:03 a.m. Rupert stops by Stewart's office. The head of foreign exchange trading desk reminds him to keep a close watch on his large position, which already has a £785,000 paper profit. Rupert confirms his plan to close it by no later than next Wednesday, following some announcements he expects at the end of the G-8 Summit this weekend.

9:16 a.m. Glancing at the Reuter screen, Rupert notices a newsflash of a possible explosion in London.

9:22 a.m. Another newsflash says that there may have been explosions on three different Underground lines. Should he take whatever profits he can capture and get out? Aw, there is probably nothing very significant about any explosions, if indeed they happened, he thinks.

10:15 a.m. *There is a confirmation of bombs on three Underground trains and a newsflash of another explosion on a bus in Central London.*

11:18 a.m. *London Metropolitan Police Commissioner Ian Blair confirms six explosions on a bus and at Underground stations, and he calls the situation confusing.*

Stock markets are chaotic. FTSE 100 index is down 200 points. Foreign exchange markets have a lot of activity without any signs of a panic. But Rupert is very nervous; his position is down to a paper loss of £327,000. His first large bet . . . will it become a blot on his career? Should he take the loss and get out now?

11:38 a.m. *Rupert is still trying to absorb the potential impact of the news when his thoughts are interrupted by the booming voice of Stewart over the intercom: "Listen up, everybody. We've been asked to evacuate the building. No time for any trading as we have only about ten minutes. But before you leave your desks, I want all of you to close out your net positions by transferring them to the bank's desk in Paris or the early morning desk in New York. So let's get on with it, boys! And one more thing: Take the stairs—no lifts."*

12:05 p.m. *As the last trader is leaving his desk, an image of Prime Minister Tony Blair flashes on the TV screen with a statement regarding a "series of terrorist attacks in London" and his plans for an immediate return from the G-8 Summit in Gleneagles, Scotland.*

Leaving the building, Rupert can't avoid the sinking feeling . . . his first big bet and he can't do much about it now! Mabels Tavern and pints of lager are the farthest things from his thoughts.

Quick thinking by Stewart? Or a set of preplanned actions by the bank to blunt the impact of an extreme operational event?

A historical, fictional account of 7/7: London, July 7, 2005

The Need for a New Approach to Tail-Risk Management

CHAPTER 1

Sustainability Management is Critical

Contents

1.1. DISCIPLINED EMPHASIS ON PROTECTION FROM EXTREME OPERATIONAL RISK

Today, following the experiences of 7/7 and 9/11, no financial institution can envision not having a set of preplanned actions or Business Continuity Plans (BCPs) to mitigate the impact of extreme exposure from operational risk of a major business interruption. In fact, it is a regulatory requirement, and financial companies have invested hundreds of millions of dollars into developing, implementing, and managing BCPs. As a result, while it cannot be completely discounted, thanks to the confidence in BCPs, the exposure from an extended interruption at a major location is not considered a life-threatening situation for a financial institution.

1.2. NO SIMILAR EMPHASIS ON PROTECTION FROM EXTREME FINANCIAL RISK

There is much larger exposure—perhaps with higher probabilities—from tail financial risk that can threaten a financial institution as a going concern. Yet financial institutions often do not have a set of preplanned operating or

3

corporate activities—akin to BCPs—to blunt such exposure. Unlike BCPs, in which every effort is made to leave no details to chance, predefined activities—if they exist—to blunt the impact of tail financial risk do not include elaborate and specifically defined plans nor, unless explicitly planned, can they be readily implemented.

1.3. ABSENCE OF OBJECTIVE PARAMETERS ACCOUNTS FOR THE LACK OF PROACTIVE EMPHASIS

It is not that institutions do not think of tail risk or extreme exposure. It is just that there are no objective measures to quantify exposure from extreme tail financial risk. And it is human nature that, unless defined and quantified in tangible terms, people tend to think of things in the abstract. Without an objective definition and quantification it is difficult to develop explicit policies clearly stating what is acceptable, what specific preplanned actions may be initiated in case of an extreme event, or who is authorized to trigger such actions. It is even more difficult to define explicitly what would trigger such preplanned actions because without quantifications there are no obvious objective parameters.

Operational risks deal with physical events that leave no doubt as to when to invoke a contingency plan. In the fictional account outlined in the prologue, it was clear to Stewart that there was an interruption in their daily operational activities, which called for an immediate need to do something about it ... or else!

How do you establish an objective trigger for an extreme tail financial risk event? Should a financial institution have triggered counteractions in 2006 ... or in 2007 ... or even in early 2008? Yet triggers are essential if a contingency or backup plan is to be meaningful.

1.4. DO REGULATORY REQUIREMENTS ADDRESS EFFECTIVE MANAGEMENT OF TAIL RISK?

In the financial services industry, regulatory developments generally become the impetus for new safeguards. However, sometimes the intensity of this impetus can be mistaken in relation to what it really does or does not address. It can also lead institutions into thinking—mistakenly, perhaps—that by meeting the regulatory requirements they are managing the extreme tail risk adequately. Three such recent developments have drawn attention and are often mentioned in the context of extreme financial risk and the going-concern sustainability of a financial institution. However, as discussed ahead, none addresses effective management of tail risk.

1.5. STRESS TESTING

Following the crisis of 2008, every major financial institution is required to go through stress testing. While a step in the right direction, stress testing does not go far enough in managing the going-concern sustainability of an institution. There are two reasons for this: (1) stress testing is based upon subjective assumptions and scenarios, and (2) stress testing is designed to meet regulatory objectives, which may not necessarily always align with objectives to maintain the going-concern integrity of an institution. In addition, an unintended consequence of regulatory stress testing may actually be an increase in other elements of risk.

1.5.1. Subjective Scenarios

Stress testing is designed to test how an institution would fare under certain subjective scenarios. Such scenarios may seem quite stressful compared to normal circumstances, but they are definitely not representative of the most extreme events. The fact is, as the crisis of 2008 showed, no one can be certain of what extreme events an institution may face.

Planning grounded in subjective scenarios is like having a BCP that only provides for counteractions to certain specified events, rather than spelling out counteractions needed if there is a disruption of operations regardless of the cause of the interruption. Anyone thinking about the history of mankind knows that every major disaster has been a result of unpreparedness caused by a failure of imagination and planning for extreme events. After every major disaster—whether Katrina, Fukushima, 9/11, or 7/7 in modern times, or the rout of Napoleon's army in Russia and the sinking of Titanic over 100 years ago, just to name a few—people have always said: "Who would have thought that …!" Therefore, basing an institution's plans to deal with extreme financial risk—which can mean the difference between life and death of the business—on a subjective set of scenarios is not adequately prudent. This constitutes a fundamental and critical shortcoming of the stress-testing approach to tail risk.

1.5.2. Different Objectives

Stress testing addresses regulatory objectives, not necessarily going-concern objectives. Regulatory objectives relate to the preservation of the financial system, prevention of systemic problems, and minimizing taxpayer costs; going-concern objectives, on the other hand, must address the ongoing integrity of an institution. There is a significant gap between these objectives. For example, an orderly liquidation of an institution may accomplish regulatory objectives as has happened when many distressed financial institutions—such as Bear Stearns, Wachovia, or Washington Mutual—were taken over by another entity. In each such event, investors incurred huge losses because the institution stopped being a going concern by the time of its takeover. Because of this gap between regulatory objectives and going-concern objectives, scenario-based stress testing doesn't go far enough to address extreme tail risk and going-concern sustainability, which must be the focus of an institution.

1.5.3. Unintended Consequence

A regulatory requirement is generally viewed by the industry as a restrictive mandate that financial institutions must live with. Given human nature, experience has shown that this encourages institutions to create ways around the restrictive mandate—often through complex transactions—to continue with the agenda an institution may perceive to be in their interest, while appearing to meet the regulatory requirements. Generally, such ways around the mandate are hard to scrutinize through standard regulatory reviews, while adding complexity and possibly another dimension of risk. For example, it is doubtful that anyone considered the institutions that failed in 2008–2009 as undercapitalized by regulatory standards before 2008, and yet they failed while meeting regulatory requirements. Adding complexity to meet regulatory requirements makes it difficult to achieve the original regulatory objective and often can lead to complacency.

1.6. LIVING-WILL PROVISION

Another recent regulatory requirement calls for financial institutions to develop living wills. By outlining how a failed institution's business, posi-tions, and obligations would be liquidated in an orderly manner, a living will is meant to alleviate systemic risk *after* an institution is no longer a going concern. While useful in limiting the contagious systemic impact of a failed institution, such a provision does nothing to preserve the going-concern sustainability of an institution.

1.7. LIQUIDITY RESERVES

Maintaining adequate liquidity reserves is another regulatory requirement. This is very useful if the whole marketplace freezes up and liquidity dries up for a limited period, similar to what happened in late 2008. However, such liquidity reserves do not address the real going-concern issue for the following reason.

It is well known that the financial institution model is fundamentally based upon the illiquidity of borrowing short and lending long. This works only because it is based upon marketplace confidence. This inherent illiquidity built into its business model means that a financial institution could never maintain adequate liquidity reserves if there is a loss of confidence in the marketplace.

A crisis can quickly turn the confidence-based liquidity model into an illiquid institution. By the time an institution needs to tap into its liquidity reserves to allay a confidence problem, it is often too late and the marketplace begins to suck the remaining liquidity out of the institution. Bear Stearns, Lehman Brothers, and MF Global had extreme liquidity crises before their collapse because the marketplace stopped believing in them as going concerns and lost confidence. So if there is a confidence problem, no amount of additional liquidity reserves can help preserve a going concern because of the fundamental nature of its business model. In fact, it's the other way around. Preserving the marketplace confidence in a going concern makes adequate liquidity available.

In order to maintain the marketplace confidence, an institution must be perceived as capable of sustaining as a going concern at all times, and particularly through a financial crisis. And, to sustain through a financial crisis with confidence, an institution needs a set of disciplined pre-planned activities, or an effective sustainability management plan, that prevents extreme events from turning into a life-threatening liquidity crisis … just like the BCPs are designed to prevent extreme events from turning into very expensive or life-threatening operational interruptions.

1.8. GOING-CONCERN MANAGEMENT AND TAIL RISK

Profits may go up or down, the earnings record may be outstanding or mediocre, and the return to shareholders may be excellent or sub-par, but a financial institution should never be in a position where the exposure from an extreme event or tail risk can adversely impact the sustainability of the institution as a going concern and thus turn into a crisis of confidence. This is the purpose of effective sustainability management or tail-risk management.

1.9. IS THE NEED FOR TAIL-RISK MANAGEMENT NEW?

Banking has been around for centuries, and there have been bank failures before. Except for cases involving fraud or financial misconduct, bank failures have always been caused by problems with tail risk. Yet compared with the urgent and continuing focus on it today, it seems that tail risk didn't cast the same long shadow previously as it has following the last crisis.

Has something changed? If tail risk is always the culprit, then how was it addressed previously?

CHAPTER 2

Tail Risk is the Culprit
Tail Wagging the Dog?

Contents

> Credit policy function used to be a shield against extreme risk when credit was the primary financial risk at financial institutions. But with the proliferation of market risk, there has been a relative decline of the tail risk watchdog function in relation to the total tail risk. This has made financial institutions with large market risk more vulnerable to exposure from extreme tail risk.

PROLOGUE

Following the beautiful weather of the previous day, it seemed like a pretty dull start to a day, with sprinkles off and on that morning. There was a chill in the air, with the morning temperature in the low 40s. The city that never sleeps was up and getting started, when someone may have muttered:

"Hey, isn't that Lew Preston, president and CEO of J. P. Morgan? And over there, isn't that Charles Sanford, president of Bankers Trust walking this way? And there is Paul Volcker, chairman of the Federal Reserve Board. Here comes John McGillicuddy, chairman of Manufacturers Hanover Bank. There across the street—stepping out of a car—is Tom Theobald, vice chairman of Citicorp. Isn't that Walter Shipley, president of Chemical Bank, coming to the same building? There goes Thomas Labrecque, president of Chase Manhattan Bank. Over there, isn't that Sam Armacost, president of Bank of America? That's Tony Solomon, president of the Federal Reserve Bank of New York. Over there, that's Gerry Corrigan, president of the Federal Reserve Bank of Minneapolis. There's Bill Isaac, chairman of the FDIC. And isn't that Todd Conover, comptroller of the currency? What's going on?"

Managing Extreme Financial Risk

Actually, the sighting of any one of them — titans of the financial industry—wouldn't have been that unusual in downtown New York. However, all of them at one place? But hardly anyone noticed. Considering that all the bigwigs of the financial industry were there, someone may have asked how come no one was there from Continental Illinois Bank—a peer of this group by size? Actually, that was not an oversight.

And the meeting was not to celebrate something; the mood was far from celebratory that morning, on May 16, 1984. Following a discussion over lunch the previous day with Bill Isaac, Todd Conover, and Don Regan, secretary of the treasury, Paul Volcker had requested this early morning meeting. It was called to plan the rescue of Continental Illinois Bank.

It would have been natural for someone to say: "Hey, wait a minute! Continental Illinois Bank? Isn't that the 7th largest bank in the country? Just over five years ago, didn't Dun's Review name it as one of the five best-managed companies in the country? Didn't a Salomon Brothers analyst, barely two years ago, call it 'one of the finest money-center banks going'? And just four months ago, the bank announced earnings of $25 million and paid a dividend of $.50 per share in the 4th quarter of 1983!"

Actually, the seeds for the looming disaster were sown a few years before, when the fortunes of Continental became somewhat tied to the events in the late 1970s in Oklahoma City, OK. Following the oil crisis of 1973, crude oil prices began their upward climb from around $3.50 per barrel in 1971–1972 to over $37 per barrel by 1980. The oil industry, often mentioned as the energy sector in the banking world, was hot. Penn Square, a small bank in Oklahoma City, decided to catch the wave by making energy-related loans in amounts disproportionate to its size and capital base. Its loan portfolio grew from about $35 million in the mid 1970s to over $500 million by 1980. This was only what was on its books. Actually, it originated a much larger volume, and sold them as "loans participation" to other banks.

By the mid-1970s, Continental Illinois was a successful large bank with solid conservative roots in the Midwest. Beginning in 1975, it embarked on an aggressive growth strategy too. The energy sector provided the wave it rode to become the seventh largest bank in the United States. By 1981, it was the largest commercial and industrial lender in the United States.

One thing made Continental unique in comparison to other large banks. New York and California banks had extensive branch networks, allowing them to have a very large portion of their deposits from their branch network. State banking laws restricted a bank in Illinois to only one branch. Therefore, a very large portion of Continental's deposits—over 80% by 1982—came from the CD market, which—because of its global reach—attracts tremendous amounts of liquidity, but is also very rate-sensitive and volatile in uncertain times.

After peaking around $37 per barrel in 1980, crude oil prices began a sustained decline that caused the collapse of the energy sector as the crude prices dropped to *around $30 per barrel by 1982. The loans that were made in anticipation of high oil prices, and which fueled the growth in profits, turned sour. In July 1982, Penn Square Bank failed because of huge losses from the energy sector. This impacted other banks, such as Continental. Continental's energy loan portfolio was in trouble not only because of its own originated loans, but also because it had to recognize almost $500 million in losses on the loans purchased from Penn Square. By the summer of 1982, the problems were quite evident. In August 1982, Continental's credit rating was downgraded, and its share price declined by over 30% to $16 per share.*

The financial environment was not looking good. The Penn Square failure, accompanied by the Lombard-Wall bankruptcy and the Mexican and Argentine debt crises, had made the market very nervous. Several other large companies, such as International Harvester, were struggling. Continental had significant exposure to all of them. Somehow, Continental managed to survive the crisis in 1982–1983 and began a comeback, with its share price reaching $26 per share around mid-1983. However, despite the confidence expressed by the markets, the problems at the bank were not abating. Nonperforming loans had continued to grow. Even though the bank reported a profit in the 4th quarter 1983, it was done only with the help of one-time gains on asset sales and supported by profits from its credit card business. Things were looking grim, and the morale was pretty low. One of the news reporters noted an example of gallows humor among bank employees: "What's the difference between the Titanic and Continental Bank? The Titanic had a band!"

By May 1, 1984, questions surfaced about Continental's going-concern ability and fueled the nervousness of large depositors, with Penn Square losses still fresh in their memories. Barely two years ago, the regulators had not come to the rescue of Penn Square, and its large uninsured depositors had suffered huge losses. To address the rumors, on May 8, Continental issued a press release denying any possibility of bankruptcy. This had the opposite of the intended effect, with the Japanese and European institutions withdrawing large amount of funds from the bank. On May 10, the Comptroller of the Currency, after consultation with Continental, issued a press release that it was "not aware of any significant changes in the bank's operations, as reflected in its published financial statements, that would serve as a basis for these rumors." Once again, the statement—meant to calm the nervousness— had the opposite effect. By next morning—Friday, May 11—it was clear that something drastic needed to be done. By afternoon, the Fed announced a line of credit of $4.5 billion from 16 banks. However, by Monday morning, nothing seemed to be working for Continental, and the run on its deposits was picking up momentum. The market's view was that Continental was not a going concern anymore.

Regulators recognized that the Continental problem was not like any other bank failure. Penn Square—for example—was allowed to fail with losses for uninsured depositors. This could not be allowed for Continental because a large part of its deposit base came from 2,300 other banks and financial institutions in the United States, Europe, and Japan. More than 40 percent of them had invested funds at Continental in excess of the FDIC's insurance limit of $100,000. The FDIC knew that

66 of these banks had more than 100 percent of their equity capital invested in Continental, and an additional 113 banks had between 50 and 100 percent of their equity capital invested in Continental. Letting Continental fail will not only result in a huge cost to the FDIC to cover the insured depositors, but it could impact other banks with uninsured deposits at Continental in such a way that by one estimate it could mean over 100 other bank failures. This could result in a financial panic and cause runs on other large banks. In other words, Continental was too big to fail, as its contagion effect could lead to a large systemic problem.

With this backdrop, the meeting of the industry titans was called on the morning of May 16, 1984 to plan the rescue of Continental Illinois Bank.

2.1. CREDIT POLICY: A WATCHDOG FUNCTION WITHOUT ANY GLAMOR

Credit policy used to be and still is a critical function at financial institutions. At some institutions, it may be referred to as credit risk management. Traditionally it has lacked the glamor sometimes associated with lending departments, where loan officers and account managers are seen wining and dining clients. Nor are the credit policy personnel regarded as rain makers like the ones doing deals or bringing in trading profits. But they play a vital role.

As the name implies, this function establishes policies and monitors their adherence for prudent management of credit, which has been—and still is, at many banks—the primary source of revenues for financial institution. This involves not only developing operating procedures for evaluating and approving credit transactions, but also establishing criteria and limits for individual transactions and monitoring the credit quality of the institution's portfolio. The quality of the credit portfolio often used to be an indication of the credit policy discipline of an institution. The credit policy function does not get involved in approving individual loans, except perhaps very large transactions or the ones requiring exceptions from the established policies.

Historically, one critical responsibility for the credit policy function has been to help the senior management establish and monitor limits on the credit exposure concentration for the institution. This may not sound all that critical, but it plays a very important role in managing tail risk. Recognizing that exposure from individual transactions adds up, it is imperative to diversify an institution's total exposure to any one industry, geography, or credit segment, or a handful of transactions. The concentration of exposure by itself is not harmful, but it defines the institution's vulnerability to unfavorable changes in the external environment. Limiting concentration to any single source of exposure can reduce the impact of an economic downturn on the institution. Therefore, traditionally financial institutions have relied on diversification to manage the cumulative exposure from tail credit risk. The credit policy function is vital to managing and highlighting this diversification of tail risk.

All this may sound obvious and a no-brainer, but history is full of examples in which, in the quest for revenues, the problem wasn't only that the quality of credit was low. In many cases, the concentration of credit exposure was also high. Low credit quality by itself doesn't necessarily harm a financial institution; however, combined with undue concentration, it can do real damage in rough economic times.

Almost all bank failures of the pre-2000 era—other than the ones involving fraud or financial misconduct—could be tied to a weak credit policy function. According to an FDIC report, *An Examination of the Banking Crises of the 1980s and Early 1990s Volume I* (p. 35): "... although banks that failed had generally assumed greater risk before their failure, many other banks with similar risk profiles did not fail. In the case of these surviving banks, the effects of risk taking ... were apparently offset by other factors, including superior risk-management skills. The absence of these offsetting factors should therefore be considered more important causes of bank failures."

2.2. CREDIT POLICY ROLE AT CONTINENTAL BANK

Much has already been written about Continental Bank's problems in the early 1980s. So only a perspective that relates to three significant failings of its credit policy function is outlined here. The first is the failure to establish and monitor the credit quality. The second is a weak administration of loans. And the third is about having "all eggs in one basket" or concentration of risk. The following is based upon a discussion with Craig Carpenter who, following a 34-year career at Continental Bank, retired as vice president in 1994.

> In 1982–1983, Craig was involved with the Penn Square situation at Continental Bank to interface with the Office of the Comptroller of the Currency during their review of loans at Continental's Office in Oklahoma City, OK.

> Craig joined Continental Illinois Bank because of its reputation after receiving his MBA from Indiana University in 1960. Driven by conservative principles and steered by David Kennedy, who went on to be the secretary of treasury and then the US ambassador to NATO in the Nixon administration, Continental was on a path to become a highly respected major bank by 1975.

> However, under a new regime, the bank changed its course. Starting in the late 1970s, lending opportunities were segmented three ways. Low-return business

didn't appeal to the new regime and was not pursued. Medium-return business was mildly pursued, but the management viewed it as not the best use of its capital. Until 1982, Craig was a manager dealing with this business. And then there was the energy sector, which was hot because of the reasoning that oil, being a finite commodity, would only see its prices climb higher. Growth frenzy followed, pursuing energy loans everywhere, and there seemed to be plenty of action in Oklahoma. In addition to making its own loans, Continental found a willing partner in Penn Square; lending business had become reminiscent of the old wild-west days.

Generally Penn Square's loans fell in one of two categories. The first category included loans for prospecting and exploration, which can only be equated to the roll of a dice and should not belong in a bank. The second category included loans for deep drilling, which (because of its higher cost) could only be supported by high oil prices. This category included loans to buy rigs, which in many cases included borrowers with little to no previous experience in oil drilling. In fact, the demand for the loans in energy sector was so strong that Penn Square resorted to selling participations in loans to other lenders. Penn Square found a buyer in Continental Bank, who would take, in a number of situations, 100% of such loans, making Penn Square, for all practical purposes, a loan production unit of Continental.

Penn Square was so busy growing that in many cases documentation was deficient. So when the bubble burst, it was like a sudden destruction of the values underlying most loans. In many cases, borrowers simply walked away, abandoning drilling rigs and other equipment in Oklahoma's countryside. This image of tattered countryside in Oklahoma pretty well portrayed Continental's loan portfolio.

Buying badly underwritten loans, without much due diligence, is a problem for any bank. However, most banks can probably absorb a big hit if that is the only problem. But Continental Bank's collapse showed that a concentration of exposure is like a ticking time bomb.

Perhaps watchdog is a better word to describe the traditional credit policy function. The watchdog function's objective is to avoid the fates of Continental Illinois and Penn Square. Therefore, traditionally credit policy function plays a key role in monitoring and managing credit tail risk at financial institutions. Relatively speaking, that was easier when credit risk was the primary financial risk of the institution.

2.3. EVOLUTION OF REVENUE MODELS AND THE WATCHDOG FUNCTION

Over the last couple of decades, the revenue models of large financial institutions have changed dramatically. There are two factors that relate to how these changes have impacted the management of tail risk.

- With the increased securitization, today's financial institutions derive a much larger proportion of their revenues from market risk than in the past. This has profoundly changed the composition and the magnitude of total tail risk at many institutions.
- The complexity of the market-risk-driven revenue model has made it difficult to understand, monitor, and manage tail risk.

These factors have increased the need for a greater role for a tail-risk watchdog. Most institutions have responded to this need by enhancing risk management function, which over the years has evolved into a sophisticated discipline. However, traditional risk management function lacks the needed focus on tail risk, as we will review in Chapters 3 and 4. The net effect has been that, while the evolution of revenue models has increased tail risk, the watchdog role has not kept up with its critical need. As a result, most financial institutions are more vulnerable to extreme tail risk now than they were many years ago. A combination of this vulnerability and the bursting of the bubble contributed to blind-side blows and, in some cases, failures in 2008–2009.

2.4. COULD THE PROBLEMS OF 2008 HAVE BEEN AVOIDED?

Could a strong credit-policy-like watchdog function, focused on total tail risk, have avoided some of the problems when the bubble burst? It is impossible to answer this question because there was no one factor that contributed to the crisis in 2008–2009. But it could have certainly reduced the pain for some institutions.

So how do you manage tail risk?

Unless exposure from tail risk is addressed proactively, the financial industry that should be growing with confidence will remain burdened by the threat and anxiety of another crisis, with the tail wagging the dog rather than, as it should be … the watchdog minding the tail!

EPILOGUE

The May 16, 1984 meeting continued past the departure of Paul Volcker, who had to get to the Upper West Side to receive an honorary degree at Columbia University's commencement. Despite the looming crisis, it was critical to maintain an appearance of normalcy at the Fed to avoid any more panic in the financial system.

On May 17, 1984, following a 6 a.m. meeting of the same group, in a joint press release with the Fed and the Office of the Comptroller of Currency, the FDIC announced a package of interim assistance that included an explicit guarantee to fully protect all depositors (insured and uninsured) and other general creditors of Continental Illinois Bank.

On September 26, 1984, the FDIC implemented a permanent assistance program and thus became the largest shareholder of Continental. A new chairman of the board and a new CEO were named who began the clean up of the mess from the aftermath of Continental's downfall.

On July 27, 1987, Tom Theobald took over as Continental's CEO. He embarked on the successful rebuilding of Continental under the majority ownership of the FDIC.

On June 6, 1991, the FDIC sold all of its stock holdings of Continental Bank for a net gain of almost $200 million.

On January 28, 1994, BankAmerica announced an agreement to acquire Continental Bank.

The FDIC's total cost of the assistance, net of dividends and gains on the shares of Continental Bank, was calculated to be $1.1 billion.

REFERENCES

FDIC, History of the Eighties—Lessons for the Future. Available at: http://www.fdic.gov/bank/historical/history/index.html.

CHAPTER 3

Need for a Distinct Focus on Tail Risk
In No Uncertain Terms

Contents

> Tail risk arises from uncertainty that is at the very least hard—and maybe impossible—to quantify. Risk management addresses only quantifiable uncertainty. Therefore, a starkly different approach—sustainability management—is needed to deal with unquantifiable uncertainty.

Tail risk has been around forever. However, it has not received much attention in the financial industry in the past as extreme crises were very rare and lacked the depth and the scale of what we have come to think of as an extreme crisis today. The events of 2008—and the frequency of the threat of another extreme financial crisis since then—have changed that. They have highlighted the need for addressing tail risk proactively.

A new approach to tail risk—distinct from traditional risk management and capital management—is essential to address critical life-threatening institutional issues highlighted by the last crisis. The suggestion of a distinct approach departs pointedly from how the industry has traditionally addressed risk. Therefore, let's first review why a distinct approach is needed, as understanding the underlying reasons will help guide the development of a new approach. We will do this by turning to a basic primer.

3.1. WHY A DISTINCT APPROACH?

3.1.1. Financial Institutions Operate in the Context of Known Risk That Can be Priced

Every revenue model requires managing risk prudently. However, for leveraged financial institutions, where financial risk primarily drives the revenue engine, managing risk has a life-and-death implication.

Banking has always been about evaluating the risk of financial investing and then, taking into account—implicitly or explicitly—the probability of the loss of principal, pricing transactions in such a way as to cover the expected loss value, expenses, and a profit margin. Expected loss values can be converted into the required risk premium. As a result, financial institutions invest only when a required risk premium can be derived and priced into transactions.

Regardless of how the expected loss value is derived—via gut feel many years ago or through the extensive use of quant models recently—financial institutions still invest only when a required risk premium can be priced into the transactions.

> **Until About 25 Years Ago …**
> …when financial modeling didn't exist, or existed only in a very crude form, investing was done by employing the gut-feel or wisdom of experienced professionals. Financial investing was almost like an art or an instinct one developed over time. Over the last 25 years, the use of historical data, quants, and statistical models has turned this into a science. Today, risk management—adding a greater degree of precision to the calculations of expected loss value—has turned the old "gut-feel" instincts into quantitative equations and pushed the boundaries of fear of uncertainty to enable transactions that may have been rejected, never dreamed of, or deemed impossible to structure before.

3.1.2. However, Uncertainty Needs Focus Beyond the Pricing of Risk

Despite the increased sophistication, uncertainty must still be addressed as the actual results are determined by how events and market conditions unfold. If actual conditions turn out to be favorable relative to the expected loss value, there are larger profits than expected; if they turn out to be unfavorable, then there is an erosion of the expected profit or even a net loss that must be offset by profits from other transactions. However, conditions may turn out to be so unfavorable that large losses exceed profits from other transactions and erode the capital of the institution; in an extreme case, catastrophic losses may arise that exceed the capital and thus threaten the going-concern sustainability of the institution. So let's look at how uncertainty, with its two components, impacts an institution and can be managed.

Risk Arises From Two Components of Uncertainty
- *Quantifiable uncertainty*
- *Unquantifiable uncertainty*

3.1.3. Quantifiable Uncertainty—Managed Effectively—Drives the Revenue Model

A basic primer in statistics indicates that the probabilities of random events can be defined and modeled if adequate data is available. This means that even though the specific outcome of any single event is uncertain and unknown, the probabilities and the expected value of the outcome can be quantified. Therefore, if adequate relevant data is available, then quantifiable uncertainty can be turned into defined expected values.

Applying this to the financial world means that expected losses from quantifiable uncertainty could be defined and quantified. This implies that the required risk premium can be derived. Therefore, the revenue model is structured in such a way as to earn an adequate risk premium or revenues over time to absorb expected loss values. And if risk premium falls short, then other operational means (if available) may be used to mitigate the shortfall to yield the required profit target. This means that expected losses and exposure from quantifiable uncertainty can be mitigated and/or priced in the normal course of running a business, and are anticipated to be absorbed by the risk premium or the revenue stream over time.

This makes risk premium the primary loss-absorbing agent, or the driver of protection against expected losses. If the risk premium is priced properly and the underlying models are sound, there will be adequate revenues to cover the expected losses from quantifiable uncertainty. As a result, the objective in managing exposure from quantifiable uncertainty is to *structure* (through the risk-reward relationship), *preserve* (through subsequent business actions), *and protect* (through controls) *revenues and profits from risk* to generate adequate risk premium. This is the objective of traditional risk management, with a goal to leverage the uncertainty to maximize revenues, while mitigating and absorbing expected losses.

With prudent guidelines and limits, accompanied by proper controls, this goal drives the revenue engine most of the time. *Most of the time ... but not always!* And this is where unquantifiable uncertainty can disrupt a smoothly driven risk-management revenue model.

3.1.4. Unquantifiable Uncertainty—if Not Managed Effectively—Threatens a Going Concern

There is a small segment of the risk/exposure spectrum where, unlike discussed previously, the uncertainty cannot be defined and quantified. And since the uncertainty can't be defined, this small segment of the risk/exposure spectrum can give rise to unexpected losses. In addition to being unexpected, such losses can also be so huge as to be catastrophic in an extreme situation and obviously so large that they cannot be priced into transactions.

The combination of their unexpected nature and the potential enormity makes it difficult, if not impossible, to mitigate such losses in the normal course of running a business. Unless specific steps are taken, the only defense against unexpected losses is the capital of the institution. This is the defined purpose of the capital and why regulators place strong emphasis on its adequacy.

However, in extreme scenarios, unexpected losses can exceed the capital, and thus threaten the survival of the institution. In such cases, the survival depends on how well the capital is protected and preserved to maintain the going-concern sustainability. If the capital were shielded adequately, then the sustainability of a going concern would not be in question.

This makes capital the primary driver of defense against unexpected losses from unquantifiable uncertainty. As a result, the objective in managing unquantifiable uncertainty is to *preserve and protect capital from risk*. This is the objective of sustainability management (also referred to here as tail-risk management), with a goal to leverage resources to mitigate and absorb unexpected losses in such a way that the capital is always protected and preserved. With prudent guidelines, limits, and proper controls, this goal drives the going-concern sustainability of the institution.

A comparison of the impact of quantifiable uncertainty and unquantifiable uncertainty is summarized in Figure 3.1.

Figure 3.1

3.1.5. Managing Sustainability via a Traditional Risk-Management Approach is Imprudent

As described earlier, risk management and sustainability management have very different primary objectives. Risk management drives the revenue engine, while sustainability management maintains the going concern. Let's highlight key differences via a human behavior analogy with some simplistic assumptions.

Let's assume that you own a roofing business. And you know from experience that there is a 1 in 10,000 chance of a fatal defect in your product. Based upon historical data, you also know that the expected loss value of the 1 in 10,000 defect is $1 million. Your experience also tells you that you can never completely eliminate the chance of a fatal defect, but you can reduce it to 1 in 1,000,000 by investing $10 million in product improvement. Would you accept the risk represented by the 1 in 10,000 chance? Or reject the risk and invest $10 million to mitigate it?

If these statistics were the only considerations, most people would accept this risk. After all, why would you spend $10 million in product improvements to offset a $1 million expected loss value? *This is risk management* in a traditional sense, where cost–benefit comparisons and profit motivations drive decisions.

Now, let's assume that you and your spouse need to add a room to your house for your newborn baby. We will assume that, since you own a roofing company, your business will install the roof on the new room.

Should you say to your spouse: "Hon, we are going to have a nice room for our baby, but I want you to know that there is a 1 in 10,000 chance that the roof could come down and possibly kill our baby. I think we should live with this risk, as it costs too much money to alleviate it." What do you think will be your spouse's reaction? And if the spouse's reaction is not to your liking, should you add: "But Hon, we do this at the office all the time!"

Most people would agree that it is dysfunctional to think of your child's life in terms of a monetary cost–benefit tradeoff. In fact, most people would do everything they can so that their child's life is not at risk independent of cost–benefit or other financial factors. *This is sustainability management,* where existential motivations drive decisions.

Similarly, to think of sustainability of a going concern in terms of probabilities, expected values, cost–benefit tradeoff, etc. is not just dysfunctional; it is also imprudent. No responsible, prudent individual wants to leave survival to probabilities.

As summarized in Figure 3.2 and illustrated through the roofing example, risk management and sustainability management have such different objectives and motivations driving decisions that one cannot be extended to manage the other. Risk management drives the revenue engine, while sustainability management preserves the going concern. Each discipline requires its own unique management process. Relying on risk management to manage going-concern sustainability is a disaster waiting to happen, as shown by the events of 2008. Similarly, extending sustainability management to manage the entire spectrum of risk will keep an institution from maximizing financial returns associated with its revenue model. Instead, simultaneous but distinct effective management is imperative to capture the full growth potential of a business model aggressively … and prudently.

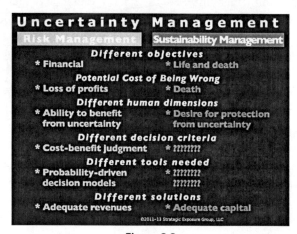

Figure 3.2

3.2. EFFECTIVE MANAGEMENT CALLS FOR A DISTINCT FOCUS ON SUSTAINABILITY ISSUES

Issues related to risk management to deal with quantifiable uncertainty and those related to sustainability management to deal with unquantifiable uncertainty are starkly different.

- Risk management has a *financial* objective, while sustainability management is about the *life and death* of the company.
  - The cost of being wrong in relation to risk management is the *loss of profits*, whereas the cost of being wrong in relation to sustainability management could be the company's *death*.
- Risk management deals with the human dimension that employs the *ability to benefit from uncertainty*, while sustainability management needs to cater to the desire for *protection from uncertainty*.
- Risk management employs *cost–benefit judgment* for decision criteria; what should be the decision criteria for sustainability management of a going concern?
- Risk management employs *probability-driven models* extensively; what tools should be used to manage sustainability?
- Risk management solutions are driven by the *adequacy of revenues* (risk premium); sustainability management solutions must be driven by the objective to *maintain adequate capital*.

3.3. SUSTAINABILITY MANAGEMENT NEEDS DISTINCT PARAMETERS

In addition to a distinct focus, sustainability management must be driven by its own parameters. Let's look at uncertainty and its quantifiable and unquantifiable components in terms of what we know and what we don't know. The known–unknown analysis divides the world into four parts, as shown in Figure 3.3: known-knowns, unknown-knowns, known-unknowns, and unknown-unknowns. We will divide the uncertainty analysis of the financial industry as discussed previously into these four parts.

- Known-knowns do not involve any uncertainty. So we will put this aside.
- Known-unknowns deal with specific outcomes that are *unknown*, but expected loss values can be quantified and thus are *known*. Therefore, risk premiums can be derived and used to manage this part of the uncertainty. *This is traditional risk management.*
- Unknown-knowns relate to the *known* scenarios we can create and for which we can gauge their impact. However, their occurrences are

Figure 3.3

unknown and cannot be defined and quantified. *This is traditional capital management*, where stress testing focuses on defined known scenarios.

- Unknown-unknowns relate to *unknown* scenarios that cannot be envisioned, and thus their occurrence is also unknown. These are the lessons we talk about after an extreme crisis in terms of "Who would have thought that …!" Physicist Richard Feynman is said to have argued: "It is not what we know, but what we do not know which we must address, to avoid major failures, catastrophes and panics." So how should we deal with unknown-unknowns? This is what *sustainability management* must cover.

3.4. THREE DISTINCT LEGS OF RISK GOVERNANCE

Risk management, capital management, and sustainability management constitute three distinct legs of risk governance. Risk management is based upon probability theory and has well-defined parameters. Capital management is based upon providing protection for projected possible extreme scenarios. Over time, certain parameters have been developed for capital planning purposes. How should the sustainability management parameters be defined and quantified?

3.5. IS THE SOLE FOCUS ON RISK MANAGEMENT PRUDENT?

Appropriately, because it drives the revenue engine, financial institutions have invested huge amounts of resources in risk management over the last 20 years. Sophisticated models have been developed. Rocket scientists have joined risk-management teams. Risk management in 2008 was a very sophisticated discipline at financial institutions. With so much investment and attention, what explains the blind-side blow to almost all financial institutions in 2008–2009? Do risk-management models have inherent limitations that keep them from dealing with the objective of ensuring going-concern sustainability?

Let's address this and similar issues in the next two chapters.

Extreme tail risk, arising from unquantifiable uncertainty, requires an approach – sustainability management – distinct from risk management and capital management.

CHAPTER 4

Sole Focus On Traditional Risk Management Can Be Dangerous

Days of Future Passed

Contents

> Risk management today is the most sophisticated discipline the financial industry has ever had. The current revenue model is also the most complex model the industry has ever had. In fact, this combination of sophistication and complexity eclipses exposure from extreme tail risk and can lead to complacency.

4.1. A MATURE INDUSTRY

There was a time not that long ago—the early 1980s, to be more precise—when many people considered banking a mature industry. One often heard that the days of double-digit earnings growth for banks were history.

The last couple of economic downturns had changed the banking environment. Higher quality credit companies had begun tapping the commercial paper market instead of turning to banks for their liquidity needs. Non-banking companies, such as GE Capital, were aggressively chipping away at the lending business. New players, such as Fidelity and Charles Schwab, were redefining consumer financial services and turning deposits into money market funds.

Banking appeared to be turning into more of a transaction processing business. Revenue growth seemed to be sputtering and, as the existing pie was being shared with new players, banks were looking beyond their traditional business to find new revenue sources. For example, at Citicorp, the three Is of Individual Bank, Institutional Bank, and Investment Bank were being expanded to five Is by adding Information Business and Insurance Business in the quest for new earnings.

4.2. A NEW DRIVER OF REVENUES

Against this backdrop, along came a unique combination of three factors:
1. *Quant* was not something that the financial industry had heard of.
2. *Securitization*, although not a common word, was somewhat familiar to some people.
3. *Computing power* was something the industry thought of only in terms of how large a mainframe computer was needed to post and process daily banking transactions.

Quants introduced rocket science to the financial industry and turned the old "gut-feel"-based art of pricing loans and investments into precise mathematical equations. Financial institutions began hiring people with new skills and backgrounds, such as calculus, statistics, physics, and chemistry: skills that were previously associated only with NASA. Information was soon dissected in every which way to turn the old yield on an instrument into precisely quantified premiums for each type of risk, and thus to create customized products to appeal to specific pools of liquidity ranging from pension funds seeking investment-grade instruments to hedge funds searching for risk to capture higher yields. With the creation of new products, including what was sometimes referred to as "synthetic instruments," there was almost no aspect of risk that couldn't be quantified and priced into new forms of transactions.

Securitization allowed financial institutions to turn almost any asset into a security that could be sold more easily in large volumes. With the increasing globalization of financial markets, securitization made it possible to fulfill the liquidity needs of borrowers in a small town in the United States from a liquidity pool in unheard of places in Sweden, Japan, or an emirate in the Middle East. Securitization greatly expanded the appeal of newly-created quant-driven products. If quants were an input for creating a reservoir of new products, then securitization created an outlet for these new products.

It is one thing to write equations and quite another to populate them with data to create a real product that can be analyzed, reviewed, bought, and sold easily in financial markets. In the fast-paced world of financial markets, huge amounts of data are useful only if they can be processed quickly and easily to populate equations and formulas. In the old world of mainframes with batch processing, this was nearly impossible in the marketplace and would have been left to the world of research projects at MIT or Cal Tech. It so happens that this period coincided with an unprecedented leap in the ability to use and manage large amounts of information as well as an enormous reduction in the cost to process information. This information wasn't measured in megabytes anymore, but in gigabytes and terabytes and soon in petabytes and exabytes.

4.3. DAYS OF FUTURE PASSED

The combination of these three factors redefined the financial industry. Driven by new algorithms developed by quants, growing computing power was harnessed to leverage enormous volumes of data to create financial instruments that could be traded in global markets through securitization. Take away any one of them, and the days of future passed would have been very different.

This combination was like strapping solid rocket boosters to a craft that was losing altitude. It lifted the financial industry into new orbits. Capital markets that were once viewed as taking away the banking business in the early 1980s became a source of new revenues for the industry. Instead of intermediating liquidity globally, the institutions began intermediating risk between the sources of liquidity and the users of liquidity: the parties who may have different views of risk from each other and thus need intermediaries to match liquidity by transforming risk. This turned the old world of the gut feel for risk into rocket science, and risk management became a very sophisticated discipline.

As it became the primary driver of a financial institution's revenue engine, risk management appropriately received an unprecedented amount of attention and resources. With such an important role, the discipline of risk management became the sole focus to recreate, manage, and drive the revenue model.

4.4. AND THEN A BLIND-SIDE BLOW

This sole focus actually became a key factor in the blind-side experience of 2008. Even though the buildup to the 2008 crisis was long in the making, no one expected such a sudden impact and the unprecedented magnitudes of the impact. Some large institutions, shaping and making markets, were gone almost in an instant. Surviving institutions were badly bruised, with some coming close to becoming casualties themselves.

4.5. A FALSE SENSE OF SECURITY

Despite the sophistication, advancement, and investment of resources in risk management, a disaster happened. Or is it that the disaster happened because of the sophistication?

In the days of future passed, enthralled by new revenue opportunities, the industry focused on what quants and models could do at the expense of realizing what they couldn't do. In the frenzy to drive revenue models, the downside was so totally eclipsed by the upside that institutions, rating agencies, and regulators neglected to focus on or even ask about the downside. With each passing year without even a mini crisis that may have highlighted the limitations of quant models, the industry developed a false sense of security. The downside was often equated, not to a crater, but to less upside.

4.6. MISPLACED USE OF MODELS

Prior to quant models, bankers and investors employed gut feel, developed from their historical experiences, and a few quantitative indicators to assess an investment or a transaction. Clearly, this had limitations as only so much information could be processed in one's head or on paper to draw conclusions and make decisions. Quantitative models and the readily available computing power changed that. This combination turned not some but all the available data from historical experiences into precise models providing key input for decision making. It created new business opportunities and fueled the risk management discipline. It also led institutions and watchdogs to take the sophistication that replaced the gut-feel sense with precise answers to mean something that these models do not do.

Professor Emanuel Derman, a physicist, is the director of the Columbia University's program in financial engineering and a former managing director and head of quantitative risk strategies at Goldman Sachs. He defines models as "metaphors that compare the object of their attention to something else that it resembles. Resemblance is always partial, and so models necessarily simplify things and reduce dimensions of the world."[1]

[1] Derman (2011)

The key word here is "resemble," as models are not capable of exactly and completely duplicating all the possibilities of the real world. At least not yet! Therefore, models have significant limitations. It is human nature that enthusiasm for sophistication can sometimes lead to a discounting of its critical limitations.

It is by design that risk management is about structuring, preserving, and protecting revenues and profits because only the large portion of the risk spectrum *can be* defined, modeled, and quantified. However, for the reasons cited previously, the knowledge and recognition of this limitation to the portion, albeit a large portion, of the risk spectrum that can be defined, modeled, and quantified was completely overshadowed by the need to drive the revenue engine. As a result, whenever someone asked about the downside from the portion of the risk spectrum that *can't be* quantified, either questions were ignored arrogantly or the answers related to the quantifiable world were assumed to apply to the realm in which their validity and usefulness is highly questionable.

4.7. MISSING FOCUS ON TAIL RISK

Let's look at the use of Value at Risk (VaR) as an example. We will briefly outline what VaR is in order to also understand what it is not. An implied extension of VaR to what it is *not* was the primary reason for complacency and a false sense of security.

VaR has been and continues to be the primary quantitative measure of market risk. There had been so much emphasis on it that it was taken as the sole indicator of an institution's market risk. But the complexities behind its definition—creating limits—were either not comprehended or were discounted. The most significant limitation is that it does not measure tail risk.

VaR is defined as the worst expected loss over a given time horizon at a given confidence level under normal market conditions.[2] Generally, annual reports of financial institutions refer to VaR as the maximum one-day loss with a 95% confidence level. So, for example, a VaR of $10 million means that an institution's loss from market risk will not exceed $10 million on 95 days out of every 100 days of operating the business under normal market conditions. In this example, VaR doesn't say anything about what the maximum loss may be on any of the other five days out of every 100 days, or what the maximum loss could be under not-normal market conditions. Maximum loss under either of those conditions could

[2] Berry (2013)

be many times the $10 million VaR amount. Therefore, not realizing these limitations and simply assuming $10 million as the maximum exposure on any given day would constitute a major oversight.

However, despite this fundamental problem, VaR was taken for granted as a solid measure of exposure from market risk. In the absence of a specific mention, it is easy to see how someone may have assumed that this included extreme tail risk. After all, it had very sophisticated science behind it! And from the prominent attention devoted to it—with detailed disclosure of data, along with how that data related to daily revenues—in any institution's annual shareholder report, one could easily assume that it was used primarily and extensively in managing market risk.

4.8. REGULATORY EMPHASIS ENCOURAGED IMPROPER USE

Actually, the use of risk-management models became so acceptable in gauging exposure from market risk that even regulators and rating agencies used them to quantify risks in an institution's portfolio. The Basel Committee on Banking Supervision allowed institutions to rely on their own VaR analysis to establish their capital requirements.

As discussed above, VaR has no direct relationship to the exposure from extreme tail risk, and the purpose of capital is to protect institutions from such extreme exposure. Therefore, the use of VaR in capital models can lead to low regulatory capital requirements if the VaR amount is low, even though the exposure from tail risk may be significantly high. In addition, the use of VaR for this regulatory purpose only advanced its acceptance at the expense of getting a handle on tail risk.

4.9. SOLE FOCUS ON TRADITIONAL RISK MANAGEMENT—DRIVEN BY STATISTICAL MODELS—CAN BE MISLEADING

According to Emanuel Derman: "Anyone who intends to rely on theories or models must first understand how they work and what their limits are. Yet few people have the practical experience to understand those limits or whence they originate."

The sophistication of quant models, accompanied by the fact that they were coming from rocket scientists whose collective expertise was beyond question, as well as the credibility lent by the appropriately huge investment by institutions, blinded people from remembering what models can and can't do. In many cases, people could not even comprehend these limitations. Models often are meant to convey one thing through "resemblance," but due to the lack of an understanding of the full picture, their meaning can become something else.

In the absence of any significant problems with revenue models in the years preceding 2008, a sense of complacency developed that kept people from focusing on the dangers underlying assumptions and what models don't do. Therefore, the perception of sophistication in what models and risk management can do contributed to: "Who would have thought that …!"

This is what happened to financial institutions in 2008–2009. The result was that institutions, rating agencies, and regulators were blind-sided. For some institutions, the price was their going-concern sustainability.

Since 2008, after recognizing the complacency that developed and the failure to fully appreciate the limitations of models, significant attention and resources have been devoted to addressing them. Some even have suggested that the problem has been reduced to a very small portion of the risk spectrum. Has enough been done to avoid the repeat of an experience similar to 2008 or even worse? Can institutions rely on probability-driven models for something as critical as survival?

> Traditional risk management is not geared to deal with tail risk. Sole focus on traditional risk management can lead to complacency, and create dangerous surprises in extreme crises.

REFERENCES

Berry, Romain, 2013. *Value-at-Risk: An Overview of Analytical VaR.* Available at: http://www.jpmorgan.com/tss/General/email/1159360877242.
Derman, Emanuel, 2011. *Models. Behaving. Badly. Why Confusing Illusion With Reality Can Lead To Disaster, on Wall Street and In Life Free Press.*

Usefulness and Limits of Quant Models

Contents

> Most quant techniques rely on linearity to drive their models, where relationships between relevant variables are stable and could be used to predict outcomes in normal times. The experience of 2008, along with other crises of the 1980s and 1990s, showed the fundamental limitation of such models, specifically in relation to their use in managing the going-concern sustainability of institutions.

Why have all the sophisticated models not been able to address the entire scope of uncertainty, and particularly the unquantifiable uncertainty that gives rise to extreme tail risk? Are there some fundamental limitations? How far can such models go in addressing uncertainty?

CHAOS THEORY AND DISASTER RESPONSE IN PERIODS OF EXTREME INSTABILITY IN THE FINANCIAL SERVICES INDUSTRY

Morton Glantz and Robert Kissell[1]

Kermit Rich, along with 30 recent MBA graduates, stood on a Long Island cliff overlooking the Atlantic. The five-acre estate promised the graduates both sun and the possibility of an invitation to join Kermit's newly charted fast-paced bank. Near the edge of the cliff, Kermit addressed the group. "My execs have enough smarts to turn quarterly profits, but their ideas lack steam to the point where our business segments behave like random walks. I need innovative products, higher risk assets, organization, not randomness in my business. I need people with guts, the kind of people that translate randomness into direction and new global banking

[1]Morton Glantz and Robert Kissell. All rights reserved.

challenges. Give me someone like a George Patton—blood, timing and guts—an executive who grabs the day-to-day stuff, makes sense of it, and is not afraid to run past goalposts. Timing aggressive bank products is everything. If you measure up, take your pick: a divisional vice presidency, healthy stock options, or, yes, I will even throw in my estate. Do any of you have what it takes?"

Kermit continued while directing the focus to the impeding cliff. "OK, you guys, inch closer to the edge. See that wicked surf crashing off the cliff. Now, if you can time your dive right and land behind one of those big waves, the surf will carry you right to my schooner. But, heaven forbid, if your timing is off, the rocks will get you 50 feet below. Blood, timing, and guts."

As the group headed toward the house, shouts echoed from below. Seconds later, a figure drifted toward the schooner.

"You're my kind of guy," Kermit said, beaming, later that afternoon. "Just name it – fast track to a divisional vice presidency? Stock? My estate?" The red-faced MBA glanced across to the 25-room mansion, and then turned to his bedazzled colleagues hanging a few feet away. "No, nothing," he replied, "Just find the jerk who pushed me over."

5.1. CHAOS THEORY GIVEN ASSUMPTION OF NORMALITY

If wave timing were predictable, the 2008 banking crisis would not have happened. One popularized wave provides some understanding of where we are today. The Kondratieff long-wave cycle (Figure 5.1) explained long-wave economic cycles. The 50- to 60-year cycle had been observed and recorded

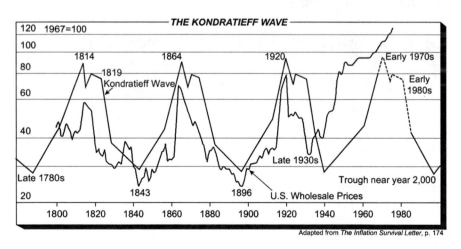

Adapted from *The Inflation Survival Letter*, p. 174

Figure 5.1 The Kondratieff wave

since the ancient Mayans of Central America. Further studies found similar long economic waves from the period of the ancient Greeks and Romans.

Kondratieff identified four distinct economic phases: a period of inflationary growth, followed by stagflation, then deflationary growth, and finally depression. Among economists who accept it, there has been no universal agreement about the start and end years of particular waves, and, of course, no perfect timing. *This points to a major criticism of the theory: It amounts to seeing patterns within a mass of statistical data that may be irrelevant in terms of predicting extreme macroeconomic shocks.* Imagine predicting a once-in-a-million-year tsunami smashing into the Long Island cliff on the spot on which Kermit Rich stood with 30 MBA graduates. Given normality, Kermit Rich would naturally build his home a safe distance from the cliff's edge to enjoy the beautiful ocean views, future tsunamis notwithstanding. But tell this to ill-prepared, shock-impervious Long Island homeowners who saw their homes washed away in a once-a-century Hurricane Sandy. Similarly, 500 poorly prepared, shock-opaque banks washed away since the extreme financial crisis erupted in 2008.

In ordinary times, business cycles, economic expansion, and recession are natural phenomena in a market economy, as natural as high and low tides and waves washing on shore. Recession is a natural mechanism of clearing the economy of inefficient economic units and a mechanism of restoring economic equilibrium after the economic-growth-induced turbulence. Unlike typical business cycles under conditions of normality, macroeconomic crisis is as unpredictable as Sandy.

Enter Basel III and the countercyclical capital buffer, aimed at achieving the broader macroprudential goal of protecting the banking sector from periods of excess credit growth and avoiding a repeat of the recent banking disaster. Banks can disproportionately expand lending in economic booms and disproportionately contract lending when the normal economy contracts. Within economic expansion waves, lending is less risky, and the Basel framework would recommend additional capital. During traditional economic contractions, lending tends to be more risky, and Basel III recommends higher levels of capital, slowing or possibly preventing banks from lending. The measures aim to dampen excess cyclicality of the minimum capital requirement by adjusting capital requirements over the business cycle. Capital requirements calibrate so that more capital is required in economic expansions than in periods of economic contractions.

Procyclicality protects the banking sector from losses resulting from periods of excess credit growth followed by periods of stress and helps to ensure credit remains available during this period of stress. Importantly, during the buildup phase, as banks grant credit at a rapid pace, the countercyclical capital buffer may cause the cost of credit to increase, acting as a brake on bank lending. Each jurisdiction will monitor credit growth in relation to measures such as GDP and, using judgment, assess whether such growth is excessive, thereby leading to the buildup of system-wide risk.

The fact of the matter is the Basel III countercyclical capital buffer is imperfect simply because economic crisis is beyond normality; crisis is inherently unpredictable and nonlinear. The characteristics of irregularity and nonlinearity reside in the field of economics, the theory of catastrophes, and the mathematics of chaos. Let us discover what the theory of chaos is about and how chaos theory provides insight into bank survival/failure odds, looking ahead to the next banking crisis.

Chaos theory refers to the behavior of certain systems of motion, such as ocean currents or population growth, to be especially sensitive to tiny changes in starting conditions that result in drastically different outcomes. Unlike what it implies colloquially, chaos theory does not mean the world is literally chaotic, nor does it refer to entropy, by which systems naturally tend toward disorder. Chaos theory relies on the uncertainty inherent in measurements, the precision of predictions, and the non-linear behavior of seemingly linear systems like stability of the US banking industry. Chaos theory studies how organized, stable systems cannot always yield meaningful predictions for a much later time, even though short-term behavior more closely follows expectations. Systems functioning in chaotic regimes may show a tendency to be highly sensitive to their initial conditions.

This means that small changes or errors can have amplified effects. Consider the "butterfly effect." A small difference, a small error, or a small change can have novel, unexpected, and even explosive effects over time. In fact, butterfly predictions may be so wildly different, they are no better than guesses. The point is, tiny changes can produce mammoth fluctuations, suggesting that a butterfly flapping its wings in Africa, an almost imperceptible event, could spark a hurricane on the East Coast. Or the approval of one home mortgage in Wisconsin could cause banks to fail all across Europe. Edward Lorenz in the 1960s completed the first computer simulations that demonstrated dynamical instability with equations and data. Which brings us to the main point: Whether or not a financial institution begins the next economic crisis with chaos and ends with chaos depends as much on management survival strategies as on the economic collapse itself. Let us dig into chaos theory and the disordered nature and timing of waves, so that we understand extreme collapse a little better.

Recall that chaos does not necessarily mean "chaotic world economy." Rather, it is associated with tons of information that hits firms daily from all directions; each piece, by itself, is "chaotic." However, data ceases to be random since patterns emerge (and relationships form) which were hidden beforehand. Bank managers maneuvering their ship in a fog of haphazard strategic plans are similar to a single sentence in a novel. They know how to form words (data) in a sentence and can read the sentence. However, they will not be able to go beyond the single sentence, and will not know how the novel turns out. The sentence—with respect to the novel—is itself chaotic. In the same way, bank policies and procedures absent of survival planning is chaotic. Think of the stock market random walk theory. It's true; while daily price movements are indeed a random walk, long-term trends (bull and bear) are not random—they are made up of pieces of trend lines. The pieces are chaotic, not the trundling taken as a whole.

Chaos, rather than being derogatory, actually refers to a beautiful organizing principle: the orbit of share price around its central core, crisis survival planning. *"The most commonly held misconception about chaos theory is that chaos theory is about disorder. Nothing could be further from the truth. Chaos theory is not about disorder! It does not disprove determinism, dictate that ordered systems are impossible; it does not invalidate experimental evidence, or claim that modeling complex systems is useless. The 'chaos' in chaos theory is order—not simply order, but the very essence of order."*[2]

Chaos theory, order, and fractals describe *new technologies* applied to corporate finance, banking, investment analysis, economics, and capital markets. It's about discovering patterns out of distinct forms of nonlinear irregularities. We can think of "dynamic" as eternally changing complex systems: physics, weather forecasting, and finance, to name a few. Chaos is in everything: raindrops falling on grass, movements in financial markets measured in minutes, paperwork atop your desk. A sample of the most famous chaos image of all, the Mandelbrot set, named after its discoverer, Benoit Mandelbrot, is illustrated in Figure 5.2. This image holds a deep fascination as it can be enlarged over and over with the same patterns emerging. From the butterfly effect, this means that the initial departure point in a system (financial or otherwise) greatly influences its course and destination. This is particularly true if banks and businesses in general are

[2]Salama and Rafat (2012).

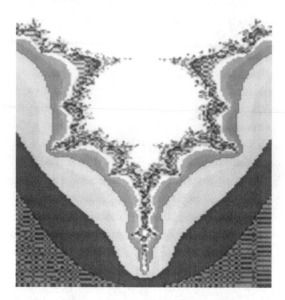

Figure 5.2 The Mandelbrot set

not properly hedged against risk of catastrophic loss. For example, firms made up of a *portfolio* of homogenous operations are less insulated against macroeconomic shocks than, say, firms who diversify operations along dissimilar businesses and operate in different regions.

While forecasting the ultimate closure of a system is as difficult as predicting Apple's stock price two years hence, it's possible to model the overall behavior of Apple's stock. We know how patterns develop within a financial system, and we often know the end result. *If we assume normality*, the issue is not a system's disorder or unpredictability, which is characteristic of any single component, but rather its natural harmonic structure. If we peered inside a microscope and examined a biological system, we'd see chaos metamorphose to patterns and harmony in systems as multifarious as Apple stock, the cosmos, a Brahms masterpiece, or weather patterns. Data packed into static equations are likely trifles, but not the dynamic, behavioral nature of our butterfly and its influence within a much larger universe. Stephen Hawking, the great theoretical physicist, agrees with the idea of chaos. He sees nature in terms of particle physics, as not fully explicable; something is missing within the theories. Hawking believes that chaos theory bridges the gap between particle physics and reality. He has stated in his book *Black Holes and Baby Universes*,[3] and in other essays, that: *"With unstable and chaotic*

[3]Hawkins (1994).

systems, there is generally a time scale on which a small change in an initial state will grow into a change that is twice as big." He goes on to say, *"predictability of a system only lasts for a short period of time."*

The key point as Stephen Hawking would have it is about time scale and evolving system dynamics. You prepare your Rhode Island textile firm's market and production forecasts by initially researching historical data. You discover that intraday sales are random, but when you stretch the time scale, they form a trend line component, the result of market, customer, and period patterns over time. The trend line established enables you to plan your firm's future. Let us connect this to fractals, geometric patterns repeated at ever-smaller scales to produce irregular shapes and surfaces. Fractals are self-similar objects, meaning single parts are linked to the whole. Fractals are used in computer modeling of irregular patterns and structures in nature.

Privet bushes are good examples. While the stems get narrower and narrower, each stem is structurally similar to larger and thicker stems, and finally to the whole bush. Similarly, you may record daily or intraday divisional sales, sales by product line, national versus regional sales, and sales contribution by customer. Next, you may move to longer periods: weekly or monthly sales. The structure (sales) at first glance may take on a familiar appearance. However, moving in, you view more detail. Repetitive patterns form, and you begin to see minute (sales) details connecting to larger structures, looking very much like Feigenbaum's fractal. Consider that insignificant dots evolve to patterns, and patterns translate to pictures. Chaotic data, like individual dots, tend to splatter around a page; that's why *linear* models do not exhibit *sine qua non* arrays of convergence.

5.1.1. Nonlinear Financial Models

Nonlinear financial models emerged from chaos theory. A meteorologist, Edward Lorenz, is credited largely with discovering chaos theory. Lorenz developed a set of 12 equations to forecast weather patterns, setting computer algorithms to move in a pattern of sequences. To save time, he ran the program at midpoint rather than at the beginning and discovered the sequence evolved in a wildly different way. It seemed that Lorenz typed in only three digits, .506, rather than the number in the original sequence, .506127.

The results that came in were unexpected. A weather forecaster is lucky is if he or she can measure accurately to three decimal places. The fourth, fifth, or sixth *dp* were well-near impossible to measure at the time, and should not have influenced the experiment in the slightest. The amount of

Figure 5.3 Lorenz's weather graph

variance in the start-up points of the two curves (in his experiment) was so small that we compare the variance to a butterfly flapping its wings (Lorenz's weather graph is displayed in Figure 5.3).

5.2. CHAOS THEORY GIVEN ASSUMPTION OF EXTREME CRISIS

This new appreciation for chaos has led to an understanding of both the nonlinearity of the world in which we live and of the functional aspects of instability as a means for adapting to new situations. Chaos is one possible result of the dynamics of nonlinear systems. Nonlinearity refers to behavior in which the relationships between variables in a system are dynamic and disproportionate. In nonlinear systems, small changes or small errors can have big effects. Moreover, in nonlinear systems outcomes are subject to high levels of uncertainty and unpredictability. In nonlinear systems, behavior is erratic and filled with surprises. Our world is filled with nonlinearity.[4]

The best way to understand how disaster and emergency events are non-linear systems is to compare the behavior of such systems with that of linear or simple systems. In linear systems, the relationships between relevant variables is stable.[5] If calamity and emergency response processes were linear systems, we could predict the number of fatalities or the amount of resources and personnel required to bring order to chaos—or prevent a bank's risk-products portfolio from collapse. We could make statements such as an 8.5 earthquake centered on San Francisco's Market Street would kill exactly Y people. We often make these linear estimates because, since the Great Depression, we have never observed a financial crisis quite like the 2008

[4]Kiel (1996).
[5]IBID.

one that caught the world by surprise. Linear tools for prediction and response limited us.[6]

The potential for nonlinearity and erratic behavior to occur in complex human environments emphasizes the overly simplistic assumptions we often make about system behavior and real outcomes. In 1992, the city of Chicago suffered a devastating downtown flood due to a failure in the city's tunnel wall. Only later was it discovered that a private contractor tried to report the failure, but no city authority responded to the report. A crack that could have been remedied for $10,000 eventually cost taxpayers, the city, and businesses an estimated $1.7 billion.[7] The nonlinear and explosive effect of a seemingly small crack led to real disaster. In disaster and emergency services management the outcomes of our errors, oversights, and even our best intentions may only, much later, result in real and unexpected surprises.[8]

Recent economic events made it abundantly clear that quantitative finance methodologies and internal risk-modeling techniques grounded on normality and historical (statistical) relationships fail to capture extreme events occurring in periods of systemic stress. Backward-looking assumptions about correlations, volatility, and market liquidity embedded in banks' VaR and other risk models did not hold up. Historical relationships do not constitute an end-all basis for forecasting grave risks. It stands that under normality assumptions, the probability of large market movements is largely underestimated and, more specifically, the probability of any deviation beyond four sigma is basically zero. Unfortunately, in the real world, four-sigma events occur, and they certainly occur more than once every 125 years, which is the supposed frequency of a four-sigma event (at a 99.995% confidence level) under the normal distribution. Even worse, the 20-sigma event corresponding to the 1987 stock crash is supposed to happen not even once in trillions of years. Extreme value functions statistically capture extreme nonlinear systems.

Take, for example, the Gumbel distribution depicted in Figure 5.4. The Gumbel distribution, named after Emil Gumbel, is a continuous distribution used in the physical sciences to model the distribution of the maximum or minimum values of a sample of data. We employ the Gumbel distribution to model extreme events. Examples include the maximum level of a river in a given year, the maximum or minimum temperature

[6]Mainzer (1994).
[7]Roeser (1992).
[8]IBID.

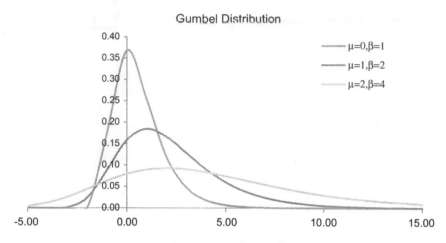

Figure 5.4 The Gumbel distribution

(for cooling and heating planning), the likelihood of an extreme natural disaster such as a flood or earthquake, and financial disasters such as the likelihood of default in an economic shock, extreme price movement, or volatility jumps. There are two standard parameters for the extreme value distribution: mode and scale. The mode parameter is the most likely value for the variable (the highest point on the probability distribution). After you select the mode parameter, you can estimate the scale parameter. The scale parameter is a number greater than zero. The larger the scale parameter, the greater the variance.

The Gumbel maximum distribution has a symmetrical counterpart, the Gumbel minimum distribution. These two distributions are mirror images of each other; their respective standard deviations and kurtosis are identical, but the Gumbel maximum is skewed to the right (positive skew, with a higher probability on the left and lower probability on the right), as compared to the Gumbel minimum, where the distribution is skewed to the left (negative skew). Their respective first moments are also mirror images of each other along the scale (β) parameter.

For illustration purposes, the mathematical constructs for the extreme value distribution are depicted in Table 5.1.

5.2.1. Extreme Event Prediction

As the Gumbel distribution demonstrates, extreme events are impossible to predict; they are singularities within fat tails, and like elementary particles, they pop in and out of existence. When a physicist refers to a

Table 5.1 Mathematical constructs for the extreme value distribution

Notation	Gumbel (μ, β)
Parameter	$0 \leq \mu \leq \infty$ $\beta > 0$
Distribution	$x \geq 0$
CDF	$\dfrac{1}{\beta} exp \left[\dfrac{x-\mu}{\beta} - exp \left(\dfrac{x-\mu}{\beta} \right) \right]$
PDF	$exp \left\{ -exp \left(-\dfrac{x-\mu}{\beta} \right) \right\}$
Mean	$\alpha - \gamma\beta$
Variance	$\dfrac{1}{6} \pi^2 \beta^2$
Skewness	$-\dfrac{12\sqrt{6}\xi(3)}{\pi^3}$
Kurtosis	$\dfrac{12}{5}$

Where: γ = Euler-Mascheroni constant and $\xi(3)$ = Apery's constant.

singularity, he or she refers to an infinitesimal but infinitely dense quantity. For example, at the center of a black hole is a point (singularity) where the laws of physics break down. Singularities are hidden, or "clothed," by the black hole, never to be observed. Extreme crisis is also a singularity: hidden, invisible, and unpredictable. If we connect the laws of physics to bank stress-testing attempts prior to the debt crisis, we find that global banks attempted to capture fat-tail risk by means of imperfect models. During the debt crisis, imperfect models like Value at Risk (VaR) severely underestimated the tail events and the high-loss correlations under systemic stress. What proved to be the most unpredictable of all was that crisis occurs more frequently, and losses are more severe, than VaR estimates have implied. VaR failures have led the Basel Committee to encourage banks to supplement VaR with a robust stress-testing program that can better capture tail events and incorporate the systemic risk dimension in banks' risk management, and that translates to extreme value functions. In fact, a 20-sigma event, under the normal distribution, occurs once every "googol," which is one with 100 zeroes after it. Thus, quantitative finance methodologies and internal risk modeling techniques based on normality will not capture extreme events that occur in periods of systemic stress. *The backward-looking assumptions about correlations, volatility, and market liquidity embedded in banks' risk models did not hold in times of extreme stress. Historical relationships do not necessarily constitute a good basis for forecasting the development of future risks.*[9]

Our understandings of how chaos theory, nonlinearity, instability, and complex patterns play out help financial institutions formulate survival plans well ahead of the next calamity. Bankers would be wise to acknowledge that nonlinearity in the world in which we live, and the aspects of instability, point out that bank management who put profits ahead of disaster survival strategies may see their institutions vanish when the next debt crisis hits.

> If survival is the most fundamental objective, then no predictive model can help manage it.

REFERENCES

Hawkins, Stephens *Black Holes and Baby Universes*, Bantam (September 1, 1994).

Kiel, L. Douglas Ph.D. University of Texas at Dallas, *Lessons for Managing Periods of Extreme Instability*, California Research Bureau, California State Library, CRB-96–005.

Mainzer, Klaus, 1994. *Thinking in Complexity*. Springer-Verlag, New York.

Roeser, T., May 28, 1992. *Chicago Flood's Lessons − Privatize.* Wall Street J, 38.

Salma, F., Rafat, H., 2012. *Tiling of Chaotic Manifold and its Fractal Folding.* J Am Sci 8 (12).

The Basel III Capital Framework: a decisive breakthrough, Herve Hannoun Deputy General Manager. Bank for International Settlements IBoJ-BIS High Level Seminar on Financial Regulatory Reform: Implications for Asia and the Pacific Hong Kong SAR, 22 November 2010.

[9]The Basel III Capital Framework (2010).

SECTION *2*

Elements of Sustainability Management

CHAPTER *6*

If you Can't Measure it, You Can't Manage it
Taming Something That's Lurking Around

Contents

Something can be managed only if it can be defined, quantified, and measured.

6.1. PREREQUISITE TO AN EFFECTIVE MANAGEMENT PROCESS

A management process requires three sound components to work effectively:
- Definition and quantification criteria
- Judgment on limits or targets
- Management controls

It is well known that unless there is a definition and quantification of a driving measure, it is nearly impossible to implement an effective management process. For example, it is difficult to manage profitability if there is no way to define, quantify, and measure profits. Similarly, risk cannot be managed to maximize earnings effectively if you can't define and quantify expected loss values. Along the same lines, it is difficult–if not impossible–to manage the going-concern sustainability and programs to protect against tail risk if there is no measure to drive this process.

6.2. AN EXAMPLE

6.2.1. Unquantified Exposure

Walter Wriston and Bill Spencer, chairman and president of Citicorp, respectively, were frustrated. Once again, Citicorp's net interest revenue had declined in consecutive months. The unpleasant announcement at the shareholder meeting in Houston TX of first quarter earnings decline of 34% from the same period a year ago was still fresh in their minds. Until recently there had been an assumption, based upon the experience of a few years ago, that when interest rates increased, Citicorp's net interest revenues would go up. Yet, in the second half of 1979 and early 1980, the opposite was happening. Sure, net interest revenues declined because interest expenses increased, but so did interest income, albeit by a smaller amount. However, knowing that alone was not very helpful as it didn't quite enable identifying specific quantifiable actions that could stem the decline in net interest margin with the increasing interest rates. And there was no near-term relief in sight from increases in interest rates.

Paul Collins, senior vice president and head of accounting and control, had his staff of financial analysts working to crunch the numbers in several ways to provide different perspectives of the same results. Interest rates on six-month CDs had climbed from around 11% at the beginning of 1979 to around 14% in the early months of 1980. It was clear that the total yield on assets was not keeping up with the increase in interest cost of deposits and borrowed funds. There had to be a way to turn the net interest margin dynamics in such a way that proactive steps could be taken to address the problem. It was clear that the company had too much exposure to interest rate changes, but how could this be addressed going forward?

In the previous few years, institutions like Citicorp had added fixed-rate mortgages and credit card loans to their asset mix. Credit card receivables created a double whammy. Not only was the interest rate charged on these receivables fixed in this rising-rate environment, most states had relatively low usury limits of 12% on credit card debt. This meant that credit card receivables on a financial institution's balance sheet were under water and getting deeper in the water with each increase in interest rates.

6.2.2. Industry-Wide Problem

Actually, the problem wasn't just confined to Citicorp. In the 1970s and early 1980s, it was common to see headlines of a significant unexpected hit to a financial institution's earnings because of an increase in interest rates. The volatility in interest rates contributed another uncertainty to a financial institution's earnings in addition to the uncertainty from credit exposure. There weren't many proactive options to avoid this volatility.

Prior to 1980, there didn't exist a measure of interest rate exposure. Managers were aware of interest rate risk, as it didn't take rocket science to know that a fixed-rate asset funded by short-term deposits or borrowings was bad news in a rising-rate environment. However, no one could simply quantify—with reasonable precision—how much of an institution's income was at risk due to the interest rate structure of its balance sheet. Because interest rate exposure was not quantified, there was no effective corporate interest rate exposure management process. The traditional approach to managing net interest margin was through asset-liability management, with a goal for the treasury function to minimize the cost of funding and to issue longer-term debt whenever the interest rate environment seemed favorable.

6.2.3. A Framework to Define and Quantify

At Citicorp, treasury functions had very elaborate control mechanisms to manage the highly decentralized funding structure with "gap management" limits on liquidity positions, but no guidelines existed to manage interest rate risk. With the growth in core deposits lagging increases in fixed-rate assets, business was becoming more exposed to interest rate changes, despite the best efforts of asset-liability management. With this backdrop, it was clear something needed to be done to manage the net interest margin more effectively.

In early 1980, Paul Collins led the corporate effort to address this critical and urgent issue. His staff created a framework to define and quantify interest rate exposure. The difference between the amount of assets repricing and the amount of liabilities repricing in a given period was defined as interest rate gap. In a simplistic way, the multiplication product of this gap and the change in interest rates during the period was the change in net interest revenue. And, by managing the structure of this gap, the interest rate exposure to the net interest margin could be addressed proactively. All of a sudden there was an actionable way to quantify the interest rate exposure.

6.2.4. Options from the Quantification

Initial findings from the analysis were not pretty at Citicorp. The good news was that there was an actionable framework in relation to changes in interest rates. The bad news was that the open-ended exposure to rising rates was very large. Another simple analysis showed that if interest rate increases matched the maximum historical increase in any three-month period over the previous 25 years, the earnings exposure was worse than could be imagined. Something needed to be done short term as well as in the long run. Reducing the gap in the high-rate environment of 1980 was not a very attractive option, but it was a better option than living with the large gap and the uncertainty of additional interest rate increases.

Now that a measure had been defined and quantified, it was clear that the current interest rate gap was unacceptable. So the questions were, what should be the acceptable magnitude of the gap, and what should be the corporate policy to manage the interest rate exposure of the institution? After several discussions, the finance committee of Citicorp developed a policy that established the limit on interest rate exposure. Several corporate programs involving restructuring of assets and liabilities were created and implemented to reduce the interest rate exposure to the policy target. Approximately 18 months later, the corporate interest-rate exposure was down to a level below the newly-established interest-rate-gap limit.

6.2.5. Risk Transfer: The Old Fashioned Way

One particular program in hindsight has an interesting meaning today. A transaction was undertaken to sell a large portfolio of fixed-rate mortgages to an insurance company to reduce the interest rate gap. The transaction provided for certain limited warranties in relation to credit losses on the portfolio. Today, one has several options to achieve the same results as delivered by this transaction in 1980. However, before anyone had heard of swaps, this transaction had the same effect as if Citicorp and the insurance company had executed a combination of interest rate and credit default swaps. In a way, this was a precursor to swap transactions that were to come in the following years.

In addition, an effective interest rate gap management process was implemented, with the result that the exposure to interest rates changed from something that was always lurking around to something that could be managed proactively. Paul Collins went on to become the head of Citicorp Investment Bank in 1983, which soon became a major global player in swap origination and trading, along with other capital market services. Following a 39-year career at Citicorp, he retired in 2000 as vice chairman of Citigroup.

6.2.6. From Something Lurking Around to Managing it Proactively

Today, interest rate gap quantification is the foundation of interest rate exposure management at all businesses. Financial institutions and other companies employ interest rate derivatives to manage their exposure. The market trades hundreds of millions of dollars of swaps without missing a beat every day. Trillions of dollars in notional amounts of interest rate swaps are outstanding globally. As a result, we rarely see headlines about a financial institution's net interest rate margin being blind-sided by interest rate movements. None of this would be possible if there were no measure of interest rate exposure.

6.3. YOU CAN MANAGE EXPOSURE FROM TAIL RISK ONLY IF YOU CAN MEASURE IT

Currently, there is no definition of a measure for exposure from tail risk. Therefore, the key challenge today is to define a measure that can be used to develop metrics related to the sustainability of an institution as a going concern. Experience shows that developing a measure not only paves the way for an effective management discipline, but can also lead to new and innovative solutions that hadn't been envisioned before.

In order to manage something, one needs to define and quantify it first. However, the measure needs to be effective and simple, particularly in capturing the complexities of today's revenue model.

CHAPTER 7

Simplicity to Counter Complexities of Revenue Models

Contents

> Complexity requires simplicity to manage it effectively. Considering the increasingly complex revenue models, it is critical that any measure of tail risk be simple.

Sustainability management requires not only a measure to drive the process; it is also critical that such a measure is simple to ensure it can be managed effectively. Anything other than a simple measure renders effective decision making difficult. If the cost of being wrong or not being aware of something can impact the survival of the firm, and effective decision making is critical, then having a simple measure that is easy to grasp objectively is as important as having a measure in the first place. To appreciate this need, let's review what role simplicity plays in decision making, both where events can be predicted (quantifiable uncertainty) and where they can't be predicted (unquantifiable uncertainty).

7.1. DECISION MAKING ENHANCED BY ADVANCES IN TECHNOLOGY

Risk management is based upon the theory of probability and thus has an implied assumption that events can be predicted. In the pre-quant era, even though all the relevant information existed (mostly on paper, or in some

53

cases on mainframe computers), there was a very low limit on how much of it could be accessed, manipulated and analyzed. Economists have always recognized this limitation. In fact, Nobel prizewinner F. A. Hayek's explanation of the market mechanism over 50 years ago was based upon this limitation. Hayek's "defense (of the market mechanism) did not rest primarily upon the supposed optimum attained by (market mechanism) but rather upon the limits of the inner environment – the computational limits of human beings."[1] Until about 25 years ago, this low limit severely restricted the ability to use historical data to manually populate models and predict events.

Over the last 20 years, the combination of easy access to historical data and growing computing power has changed this limitation into what one may describe as: if it exists, it can be accessed and manipulated. As a result, previous low limits for the ability to predict can now be pushed to an extreme. This has enabled a very sophisticated approach to decision making where the outcomes can be predicted and risk can be priced into transactions to drive revenue models.

7.2. DESPITE TECHNOLOGY AND QUANT ADVANCES HUMAN DECISION MAKING REMAINS SIMPLE

While the ability to manipulate and analyze data, and thus the scope of depth and breadth of input variables, has grown enormously, human decision making is still a very simple exercise. "A man, viewed as a behaving system, is quite simple. The apparent complexity of his behavior over time is largely a reflection of the complexity of the environment in which he finds himself."[2] For this reason, the extent of inputs a human being can handle in making decisions is still very limited. Therefore, effective decision making that employs huge databases, such as in risk management, requires turning the complexities into simpler inputs for effective human use in decision making. This is what sophisticated risk-management models do. Anything more complicated can't be effectively processed by human beings.

7.3. DECISIONS REGARDING UNQUANTIFIABLE UNCERTAINTY REQUIRE A DIFFERENT APPROACH

Despite the expansion of the predictable spectrum of uncertainty, nothing can define and quantify all probable scenarios and accurately assign probabilities. Some modern quant models claim to have an ability to predict all

[1] Simon (1996), p34
[2] Ibid, p53

events up to 99% or higher probabilities. Even if that were possible, it still leaves out that very small part of the risk spectrum which cannot be defined, quantified and predicted but is capable of causing catastrophic damage. So how does one manage the exposure from extreme tail risk where uncertainty cannot be quantified and extreme events cannot be predicted?

The inability to predict does not mean that human beings are not aware of it or can't manage unquantifiable uncertainty. It just requires a different approach. As mentioned earlier, it is not that institutions do not think of tail risk or extreme exposure, or try to manage it. They do. The question is how effectively do they manage it?

7.4. THE NEED FOR SIMPLICITY IS CRITICAL IN COMPLEX MODELS

Over the last 20 years, financial institution revenue models have become progressively more complex, making it more difficult to get a handle on exposure from extreme tail risk, particularly if no simple quantitative measures exist.

Without a measure one has to understand and interpret many complex interactions within revenue models to reach conclusions that may be perceived subjectively and differently by different people.

Today, all the information needed to deal with extreme tail risk exists. It just doesn't exist in a form that allows easy recognition and evaluation of the extreme tail risk. And since human beings can't deal with anything more than simple inputs, simplicity—something that makes it easy to recognize, grasp and understand—is paramount in measuring extreme tail risk.

Risk-management-driven models of Lehman Brothers and Bear Stearns were too complex to understand easily. To make matters worse, no simple tail-risk measures were available. As a result, there weren't any ongoing recognition and evaluation metrics to describe the growing vulnerability of these institutions in 2006 or 2007. While elaborate mechanisms were in place to project and track the profitability of each incremental transaction, there was no company-wide mechanism to gauge the institution's ability to maintain going-concern sustainability in an extreme crisis. Also, there were no mechanisms akin to smoke detectors or tripwires to provide a warning of how each new transaction was pushing the institution closer to a catastrophe.

This problem wasn't limited to the institutions that failed in 2008–2009. Just about every financial institution was blindsided in 2008 for not being able to easily recognize the problem until it was too late. This experience demonstrates the crucial need for simple metrics that can be monitored continuously.

Complex revenue models require algorithms to reduce complexities into simple inputs for human decision making. Often these algorithms employ assumptions and data to drive their logic. Therefore, the output of these algorithms, which serves as inputs for human decision making, becomes dependent upon these assumptions. In decision making, it is critical to know and understand these assumptions, as the "garbage-in-garbage-out" principle impacts the validity of the outcome. However, if algorithms employ models that are so complex that it is difficult to keep track of critical assumptions then one may not have a good grasp of real risk.

Responding to the complexity of revenue models with a complex system of assumptions and then having to interpret the results in the context of assumptions can add a new risk because one may fail to grasp the scope of the real risk.

Therefore, what is needed is often the opposite: i.e. more complex models require simpler measures to ensure that critical vulnerabilities can be easily and transparently spotted and monitored. Several industries with complex systems where an extreme event can have catastrophic consequences place great emphasis on this need for simplicity.

7.5. POST-2008 DEVELOPMENTS HAVE INCREASED COMPLEXITY

Today's banking revenue model is complex. Since 2008, institutions have been trying to get their arms around risk to avoid a repeat of the experience of the previous crisis. Hundreds of millions of dollars have been invested in fine-tuning risk management models and new reporting mechanisms. New laws have been enacted. Rules and regulations have been revamped, supplemented, and implemented. A new Basel accord has been agreed to. Annual stress testing, even with its mysterious workings, is anxiously awaited.

Net-net, much has been done. But one thing that has not been done is to establish a way to define and quantify the institutional exposure to extreme tail risk. To manage it effectively and to avoid being blindsided, it must be measured and monitored simply, easily, objectively and continuously. Almost everyone agrees on two things. First, an already complex situation has been made more complex. Second, no one is certain if significant contributing factors from 2008 have been addressed.

7.6. A SIMPLE MEASURE IS NEEDED AS RESPONDING TO COMPLEXITY WITH COMPLEXITY IS A RECIPE FOR DISASTER

Adding complexity to something that is complex and not measurable in the first place is not only futile, it can also be dangerous. Therefore, simplicity is important to avoid being blind-sided, as happened in 2008, and for effectively managing extreme tail where the cost of being wrong or not being aware of something could determine the survival of the institution.

Andrew Haldane and Vasileios Madourous of the Bank of England[3] have recently published a paper about the complexities of regulations of financial institutions. Some of their conclusions are valid for financial institutions too. One of their conclusions is that, "Applying complex decision rules in a complex environment may be a recipe not just for a cock-up but catastrophe ... Drawing on experience from a variety of real world systems – nuclear power plants, oil rigs, aircraft navigation systems – Tim Harford (2011) illustrates how complex control of a complex environment has often been calamitous. ... The general message here is that the more complex the environment, the greater the perils of complex control."[4]

Considering what's at stake, simplicity shouldn't be a luxury; it should be a critical mandate. Therefore, any new measure must be simple, despite some sentiment that today's revenue models are too complex to simplify. A simple measure can be created that enables easy, objective and continuous monitoring of exposure from extreme tail risk. Let's look at this in the next chapter.

> Just because something is complex doesn't mean it can't be simplified and thus handled more effectively. Anything to the contrary is a recipe for disaster. Therefore, it is critical that any measure to drive tail-risk or sustainability management be simple

---

[3] Andrew Haldane is executive director of financial stability and member of the financial policy committee of the Bank of England, and Vasileios Madourous is an economist at the Bank of England.
[4] Haldane and Madourous (2012)

REFERENCES

Arrow, K., 1987. *Economic Theory and the Hypothesis of Rationality* from The New Palgrave: A Dictionary of Economics. Macmillan Press, London.

Haldane, A., Madourous, V., 2012. *The Dog and The Frisbee*. Presented at the Federal Reserve Bank of Kansas City's 36th Economic Policy Symposium: The Changing Policy Landscape at Jackson Hole, WY August 31, 2012.

Simon, H.A., 1996. *The Sciences of the Artificial*. MIT Press.

CHAPTER 8

A New Measure for Effective Sustainability Management

Probable Maximum Loss

Contents

> Using established practices in the insurance industry, a probable maximum loss can be defined and quantified as a measure of extreme tail risk.

8.1. A SIMPLE MEASURE TO GAUGE THE SUSTAINABILITY OF A COMPLEX MODEL

Probable Maximum Loss, or PML, is the maximum possible loss, mitigated by reliable, predefined, and structural actions and safeguards to reduce, prevent, or offset the loss. An institution's PML is the sum of PMLs from all off- and on-balance-sheet items as well as PMLs of exposure from all of its operations. It represents a measure of maximum exposure from extreme tail risk.

An Example of PML Definition

The PML of a $10 million loan portfolio or a $10 million of notional amount of credit default protection sold is $10 million. However, if there are collaterals, backstops, guarantees, or safeguards that are designed to trigger automatically a set of reliable and predefined actions to reduce the maximum loss by $3 million, then the PML, or the maximum mitigated exposure, of the portfolio is $7 million ($10 million of maximum unmitigated exposure less $3 million of structural safeguards/backstops).

Let's construct a simple example. Computing PML is an extensive task requiring a review of data and records maintained by an institution. However, to illustrate an example, we will create a simple picture with some simplistic assumptions about the data. Figure 8.1 shows the assets of a financial institution that add up to a total of $200 billion.

We should add to this total all off-balance-sheet items that can give rise to exposure from uncertainty. To keep it simple, in our example, we will add just two such items: the notional amounts of all credit derivatives and guarantees sold by the institution. The reason we add the notional amount is due to the fact that the maximum exposure from these two items is the full notional value. This gives us a total of all assets and equivalent items of $250 billion.

Assets & Equivalent Items

Book Value in $Billions

ASSETS:	
Cash & Deposits	6
Fed Funds	3
Investments	44
Loans, net of Reserves	120
Intangibles & Deferred Tax	14
Other Assets	13
TOTAL ASSETS	200
OFF-BALANCE SHEET ITEMS:	
Credit Derivatives, Notional Amount	48
Guarantees	2
TOTAL	250

©2011–13 Strategic Exposure Group, LLC

Figure 8.1

The PML computation results of our example are summarized in Figure 8.2. The bar on the far left represents total assets and equivalent items amounting to $250 billion. The first step is to calculate the maximum amount of potential loss from each item on and off balance sheet. This is the amount of the maximum loss in extreme unfavorable conditions assuming the institution did not take any actions to mitigate the loss. It is the total amount of maximum loss structurally built into various portfolios of the institution. The total sum of these potential losses for the institution in our example is $150 billion. We will refer to this as the

"Maximum Unmitigated Exposure," which is represented by the second bar from the left in Figure 8.2.

One can think of Maximum Unmitigated Exposure as the maximum amount of the total loss in the event of a most unfavorable scenario and as if there were no personnel or managers to take counteractions to prevent or mitigate the loss. The reason it is not the full value of total assets and equivalent items ($250 billion) is because certain items, such as cash and US Government securities, are assigned zero loss values in this example, while cash or cash-equivalent collaterals may reduce maximum losses for some other items.

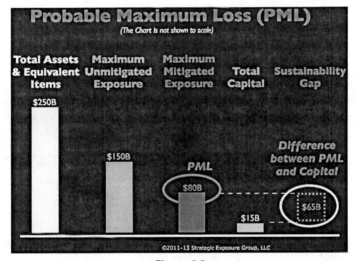

Figure 8.2

Obviously, there are personnel and managers whose jobs are not just to structure and price products, but also to preserve and protect the revenue streams from things going awry in extreme unfavorable conditions. This is called mitigation. For the purpose of calculating PML, it should not be the subjective opinions of managers as to what they think would be the amount of loss that can be mitigated. It should include only mitigations from specific plans and processes in place to backstop the loss if things go awry. These mitigation plans and processes must be explicitly defined, credible, and realistic contingency actions that include disciplined guidelines to stop the portfolio from deteriorating further. This amount of mitigation is subtracted from the maximum unmitigated exposure to arrive at the "Maximum Mitigated Exposure," which equals the PML and is represented by the third bar from the left in Figure 8.2. In our example, the maximum unmitigated exposure amount of $150 billion is offset by a total amount of mitigation of $70 billion to yield the maximum mitigated exposure or PML of $80 billion. This represents the maximum amount of total loss in the most unfavorable event assuming the institution takes all the steps to mitigate the potential loss.

In our example, against a PML of $80 billion we have $15 billion of institutional capital (represented by the fourth bar from the left in Figure 8.2) to provide protection from unexpected losses. The difference between the PML and capital is designated as the "Sustainability Gap." The institution in our example has a sustainability gap of $65 billion.

By itself, neither PML nor the sustainability gap is a predictor of survival or failure. Also, it is critical to recognize that the objective of sustainability management is not to push to close this gap, as a sustainability gap is an inherent part of a leveraged financial institution's revenue model. Instead, by quantifying PML and the sustainability gap, we have defined the challenges involved in managing the sustainability of a going concern. It is the sustainability gap and how it is managed to protect the capital that determines the strength or the vulnerability of the institution in an extreme financial crisis.

8.2. PML, AS A MEASURE OF EXPOSURE FROM EXTREME TAIL RISK, HAS SEVERAL ADVANTAGES

PML Provides:
- A common scale across varied businesses and revenue models
- The third dimension to complete a 3-D view of the risk-reward equation
- A simple measure for complex models

8.2.1. PML Provides a Common Scale

PML can be used to measure the exposure from extreme credit risk, market risk, and certain operational risks. While calculations may differ due to the uniqueness of each item's specific characteristics, all PML calculations lead to the measure of potential extreme loss, thus providing for a relative comparison of all items on a common scale.

8.2.2. PML Represents the Third Dimension, Completing a 3-D View of the Risk-Reward Equation

Imagine a world where a measure of expected loss value doesn't exist. To discriminate between transactions, all we have is a single-dimension measure of revenues. Under these conditions, it would be hard, if not impossible, to discriminate for risk and thus maximize returns and profitability for the risk-reward relationship. By adding a second dimension to measure quantifiable uncertainty through expected loss values, we can create a basis for discrimination for risk among transactions and thus can maximize profitability. This is traditional risk management, and the expected loss value represents a measure that drives the risk-reward relationship, albeit only for risk from quantifiable uncertainty.

Now imagine two transactions–transaction A and transaction B–both with the same revenue values of R and the same expected loss values of V. (For the moment, we will leave out extreme variances.) How do you simply discriminate for unquantifiable uncertainty between transaction A and transaction B to maximize financial return? They both have the same revenues of R and the same expected loss values of V. So on a two-dimensional risk-reward scale, they are identical transactions.

Now let's add a third dimension of extreme tail risk measure, as shown in Figure 8.3. On this third dimension, these two transactions have extreme tail-risk measure values of T_A and T_B. Since they both have the same values on the dimensions of revenue measure and expected loss value measure, the fact that the extreme tail-risk measure T_B is higher than T_A should lead us to prefer transaction A over transaction B.

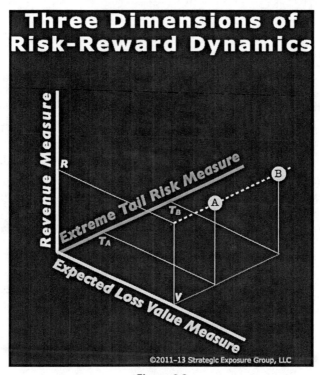

Figure 8.3

By adding a third dimension to measure PML, we can now also discriminate for the risk from unquantifiable uncertainty to maximize profitability. Therefore, PML enables us to turn the two-dimensional partial view of the risk–reward relationship into a three-dimensional ("3-D") complete view that spans risk from both quantifiable and unquantifiable uncertainties. This makes it possible to optimize a combination of three independent variables—revenues, expected loss value, and PML—to maximize financial returns.

The measure of expected losses from quantifiable uncertainty and the measure of extreme exposure from unquantifiable uncertainty are independent variables. Therefore, an institution may be very good at managing the traditional risk–reward relationship regardless of how vulnerable it may be on the PML dimension. The fact that an institution has a strong risk management function and a history of impressive profits does not by itself mean that it is in a stronger position to protect going-concern sustainability in a sudden extreme financial crisis. Conversely, if an institution is stronger than another institution in relation to extreme exposure, it does not mean it does a better job of risk management or will be more profitable. Such an institution may have a mediocre profitability and risk management record, and yet may weather a sudden extreme financial crisis better than other, more profitable institutions.

This is because revenue, expected loss value, and PML represent three independent variables. Expected loss value enables the structuring and preserving of profits, drives the revenue model of a financial institution, and is a measure of volatility of profits. PML, on the other hand, is a measure of an institution's vulnerability to extreme tail risk, and highlights the need to protect capital. It is possible to do one well without doing the other as well.

It may be possible to incorporate extreme exposure values into risk–reward equations through the use of sophisticated variance models. However, doing so would not provide simple measures for complex models, nor would it easily lead to a common scale across different business lines.

8.2.3. PML is a Simple Measure for a Complex Model

The most significant value of using PML is in getting a simple and straight answer to a simple question: *"What's the institution's exposure to extreme tail risk?"* No complex answers; no need for prerequisites that require an understanding of the complexities of revenue models; no anxiety about the scope of assumptions involved; and no hard-to-understand black-box analyses.

8.3. PML PROVIDES A SOLID TOOL FOR THE EFFECTIVE MANAGEMENT OF TAIL RISK

The combination of its ability to complete the view of uncertainty, its common scale across all business segments, and its simplicity makes PML an effective measure to quantify and manage extreme tail risk at financial institutions.

- PML, when used properly, is *the most complete measure* of extreme exposure as it is designed to cover all sources that give rise to tail risk, whether on or off balance sheet. Unlike leverage ratios, PML does not focus only on balance sheet items, nor on exposure from uncertainty driven by only financial risk.
- It is *the most objective quantification*, as it is based upon structural factors that constitute the business model, rather than driven by subjective scenarios.
- It is *simple to communicate, comprehend, and understand*, as it clearly relates to potential losses from extreme tail risk.
- It provides for a *transparent quantification* of the exposure from extreme tail risk, as there are no black-box algorithms or complex equations involved.
- It creates a *common scale for an easy comparison* of items/business lines that may have no common operational characteristics and thus may drive tail risk in different ways, as it translates exposure from all sources into a common measurement across all categories of risk.
- It is an *excellent management tool* to establish targets, limits, and guidelines because of common definition, common scale, and a manager's ability to directly control operating items that cause it.

In addition, in order to maintain sustainability through a financial crisis, it is essential to have a constant handle on the institution's exposure to extreme tail risk and not be paralyzed due to a lack of it. One often hears that in 2008 senior managers at some institutions did not have an answer to *"How bad can it get?"* Let's understand this through a few examples in the next chapter.

> PML is an effective tool for quantifying and managing extreme tail risk at financial institutions.

CHAPTER 9

Continuous Readiness is Critical

A senior executive who wishes to remain anonymous

Contents

> In today's fast-paced markets, uncertainty requires continuous readiness, which means knowing where things stand as well how to take actions to maintain control of the situation.

Investing by definition is forward looking, and forward looking means uncertainty. Therefore, investors often consider the future under several different scenarios to evaluate the risk and return tradeoff before making their decisions.

The nature of the business of finance is transactional and opportunistic. Therefore, it draws people with this inclination. Doing transactions gets rewarded, as it should. However, basic functions that require longer-term infrastructure and engineering do not come naturally to such people. While people with inclinations to build infrastructure and engineering are the ones who create such mechanisms, they are not intimately and emotionally involved in transactions, and hence there exists a gap, which can be further compounded if the relevant information is not readily available. Let me clarify this.

9.1. PLANS ARE USELESS, PLANNING IS INDISPENSABLE

For any business, plans almost never materialize exactly as they are formulated. For financial firms—operating in fast-paced markets and constantly changing environments—any specific plan dealing with market risk never materializes. Experienced managers rightly discount the value of plans, but many often underestimate the value of planning. If planning is undertaken that employs sound emphasis on key variables including consideration for effective contingencies, then managers are prepared to navigate their businesses through almost any environment. In fact, if planning emphasizes tactical flexibility within acceptable guiding parameters, then even potential disasters can be turned into opportunities to gain advantage.

What is needed is planning that gets participants invested both intellectually and emotionally. Often institutions respond with emphasis on formal plans that address only the intellectual component and only for some of the personnel involved with transactions. Hence a gap exists between what is needed and what is done.

9.2. READINESS DEFINED

Effective planning requires information and readiness, both intellectual and emotional. Being ready intellectually means having easy and timely access to relevant and critical information that has already been internalized for action. Because of the fast pace and volatility of markets, it is imperative to have the information that relates to extreme risk available on an ongoing basis to avoid the repeat of the blind-side blow of 2008.

Being ready emotionally means that all key decision makers are on the same page and understand the need for triggering contingency plans. In crises, senior managers do not have the luxury of learning and digesting new information and analyses when reactions hang on approvals, and stakeholders want updates.

9.3. DEGREES OF READINESS

Like many experienced managers in the financial industry, I have been through several crises over the last 30 years. The following are three experiences that are worth describing briefly. Each case involved a crisis, and in two cases markets were in turmoil and sentiments ranged from fear to panic. But in each case, the end result reflected the degree of readiness.

9.4. READY INTELLECTUALLY AND EMOTIONALLY

Billions of dollars of wealth was evaporating by the hour. Fear had turned into panic long before the markets opened in the United States. The nervousness of the last few days created sell orders that far exceeded buys. The futures market was significantly lower than the stock market. It didn't help that the secretary of the treasury publicly expressed concern about the falling stock prices in recent days, which only heightened the market anxiety. And then the ominous cascading wave began even before investors had gone to bed in New York. Starting in Hong Kong and Tokyo, the wave followed the sun as the day began in financial centers from East to West.

Barely four months earlier, no one would have anticipated this. The stock market was up significantly since the end of last year. Interest rates, after peaking the previous year, had begun declining. However, there had also been undercurrents causing some nervousness, as the US economy, following a couple of years of rapid growth, seemed to be shifting towards a slowdown. Policy disputes among industrialized nations were becoming more visible. Earlier in the year, a number of SEC investigations had rattled stock market investors.

The nervousness was made worse by the increasing volume of program trading. And lately, it seemed to have contributed to increasing arbitrage and portfolio insurance strategies of a magnitude not seen before, leading some people to call it an accident waiting to happen.

Over the last couple of months, PE ratios were perceived as too high, with a general consensus that the market was overpriced. Soon after the recent stock market peak, many investors had begun moving onto bonds and, in some cases, junk bonds. The lower futures market created further arbitrage opportunities, adding momentum to the declining stock market.

The day of reckoning was here! Anxiety was followed by fear, followed by panic. The markets exploded globally. No one could be sure who would survive and who would not, or even what kind of new financial problems may surface.

At a large financial institution where I was a member of the senior management team, despite some nervousness, the reaction was one of guarded confidence. Actually, the reaction had its origins many months ago. A long time ago we had initiated planning for extreme situations. Every month, extensive analytical exercises covered very extreme scenarios. It was understood that while these scenarios were unlikely, they would prepare all of us mentally for a volatile world. Severe liquidity shock, dramatic overnight change in interest rates, and other similar scenarios were considered and simulated.

As the stock market fell sharply, accompanied by an unanticipated dramatic drop in interest rates, our corporate exposure was quite evident. The anticipation of a rate-induced refinancing wave created a huge exposure in relation to the hedging strategy. All of a sudden, there was a significant imbalance in the mortgage portfolio. As had been anticipated by the scenario analysis, this created a very large net risk exposure. It became an immediate priority to ensure that the exposure was addressed. All the planning exercises of the past helped achieve two objectives.

1. *It provided for tactical flexibility, which resulted in capturing a unique opportunity to buy exotic alternate assets that were being dumped by other market players in a panic. The planning discipline led to a calm, rational evaluation of the opportunity followed by acting on it.*

2. *Because of all the planning, all decision makers were on the same page emotionally, eliminating the need for long, exhausting, stressful meetings, which often don't fully resolve the issue at hand because of the crisis mode.*

On that critical day, we didn't have long meetings, and there was no undecidedness; in fact because of the strategic thinking employed in planning, we had more tactical flexibility to implement a profitable solution.

As a result, we undertook transactions that could not have been thought of and planned ahead of time; however, thinking in contingent terms enabled us to accomplish a unique solution easily as the management team was on the same page intellectually and emotionally. The institution not only sailed through the crisis, but also made a handsome profit as a result. The readiness enabled both the management of the risk exposure and the ability to exploit the panic-induced mispricing opportunity in the market. It should also be noted that readiness by participants adds immediate liquidity to markets and helps temper the impact of panic itself.

9.5. READY INTELLECTUALLY, BUT NOT EMOTIONALLY

There wasn't much happening in the marketplace or in the political world that may have impacted the markets. The second term of the current US president was a little more than half done. The economy had been growing solidly these last couple of years. Even though there was talk of a slight slowdown, no one seemed overly concerned. Interest rates had been steady after a brief decline last year. Foreign exchange markets had been calm recently, with the US dollar continuing a slow decline versus major currencies.

Our financial institution was about to wrap up a good quarter with an estimate of a 20% year-over-year increase in net income. There didn't seem to be anything unusual to report from any of the investment portfolios or trading desks.

For almost a month, long-term interest rates as indicated by 30-year treasuries had no more than 10 basis points (bp) movement. The net position of the institution's mortgage department was anticipating a continued decline in interest rates.

After holding steady for almost six weeks, all of a sudden there was a 25–30bp increase in the 30-year treasury rate in a week. Everyone knew what an increase like that did to the mortgage portfolio. A 25bp increase may sound small, but for the mortgage portfolio, which included various securities and derivatives, including principal only (PO) derivatives, it was a concern because of extreme sensitivity to long interest rates. Senior manager awareness was spotty, as the risk had been properly documented, but not consistently reported. Week two saw another 25–30bp jump in 30-year treasury rates. The concern level shot up. The negative impact on profits was reported, which caused somewhat of a panic among senior managers. While the net impact was understood, there was a less-than-full understanding among senior managers of how the rate changes were impacting the profits and losses on the portfolio. Many lengthy discussions followed, including try-ing to find out who was at fault, but not fully understanding the economics of the situation. In one of the areas, a trader—breaching trading limits— doubled up the position, betting on decline in long-term rates. However, the following week the rates were up another 30–40bps. Now full panic set in among senior managers; because of the size of the loss, it was a full-blown crisis.

During this brief unexpected run-up in rates, the financial impact was clear, and all the information was available. However, the lack of an agreement among senior managers led to a virtual freezing of any action, with a result that by the time any action was anticipated, the loss had built up to a huge amount. It was estimated to exceed the entire institution's quarterly profits, thus creating a net loss for the quarter.

At the end of that month, the institution announced the loss in the portfolio and began an investigation. Several senior managers were asked to leave or were reas-signed within the company. At the end of the quarter, the institution reported a net profit for the quarter only because the portfolio loss was offset by other transac-tions, resulting in one-time gains. It was clear that the institution had been ready intellectually, with all the information available, but emotionally key managers were in different places, which prevented reaching critical decisions and focused more on fault finding.

9.6. READY NEITHER INTELLECTUALLY, NOR …

The winds of crisis had been blowing for months now. Actually, the nervousness had begun over two years ago when the talk of a bubble bursting had first surfaced. Stock market was months past its most recent peak. Regulatory concerns were evi-dent. Another president was winding down his second term. The secretary of the treasury was visibly involved in discussions. And yet no one knew when, where, or how the current anxiety was going to end.

Then, in a matter of less than 24 hours, everything changed as a spark started a set of cataclysmic events the likes and scope of which had not been seen in the modern financial world. In a frenzy to ensure survival, every institution was on its own. There was a total lack of confidence about the survival of financial institutions, including some of the biggest names in the industry.

The financial markets have always existed based on confidence and the ability to exchange assets among traders who understand value. This exchange creates a fair market price. So when the bubble burst and liquidity dried up, there was no exchange of assets among knowledgeable traders. The marketplace stopped func-tioning as traders began to realize that the market prices could not be reliable mea-sures of value. However, the accounting profession insisted on relying on market prices and had no contingency plan for establishing a fair price in the absence of a functioning market. No one could establish market values of trillions of dollars of assets held globally by investors that included individuals, pension and sovereign *funds, asset managers, and banks. Further, assets that were rated AAA until just days ago not only were illiquid, but it became clear they should not have been rated AAA in the first place.*

It wasn't only that the exchange of assets stopped as a result of the inability to value assets, but applying mark-to-market, based upon whatever remained of the market, the collaterals were valued at only a fraction of their value just days ago. This triggered additional collateral calls and selling pressure on already falling prices. Illiquid instruments that were valued at reasonably high prices couldn't hold their value and in many cases could not even be priced.

Rumors were flying about who may not make it. And names of who may not make it weren't limited to fledgling weak institutions. Some of the biggest names were mentioned. Almost no one was prepared for the depth of this crisis. In some cases, institutions weren't prepared at all.

Options for actions were limited. To make matters worse, no one knew how long the downward momentum would continue. Questions being asked at our institution captured the helplessness of the moment. "How bad can it get?" a senior manager asked. And it was not a rhetorical question. It was a search for any answer. However, there were no answers as the relevant information was not available, let alone an agreement on what actions to take. So being on the same page was not an option, as there was no page to be on. Through surviving a huge storm in the same boat, emotional convergence developed among senior managers, even though there was total unpreparedness when the storm began.

Finally, almost 60 days after it began, the crisis seemed to crest. During this period, all financial institutions lost tremendous shareholder value, in some cases 100% of the value. Our institution lost almost 75% of its market value during this time period. While several other institutions in the peer group have recouped a big chunk, if not all the lost value, this institution's market value is still a third less than what it was at the beginning of the crisis. Not having critical information and thus not being able to act proactively was a huge factor in the health of the institution after the crisis.

After these experiences, I became intrigued with stories of how soldiers behave under battle conditions. I came across a book titled *"Battle Leadership"* written by Captain Adolf Von Schell, based on his experiences in the German front lines of World War I. The writing was especially poignant since Schell was clearly affected by the ultimate defeat of his army. He was especially thoughtful about the psychological toll that war created. His writing reflected the overconfidence that preceded the war, the inability of the planners to anticipate the true horrors and stress of the war, and the realities of executing the war.

Schell noted the importance of explicitly training for the certainty of a confused battleground filled with stress and turmoil that could barely be imagined by those being trained. The major value of this training would be emotional stability and unity, and therefore the ability to make decisions and act under battle conditions. He repeatedly emphasized the importance of training in peacetime to prepare soldiers to make simple and clear decisions when they would surely lack adequate information to make those decisions while engaged in combat. He showed several examples to contrast the clear thinking, calm, and emotional unity that existed when units were prepared and the confusion that prevailed when units were unprepared intellectually and emotionally. In fact, preparedness allowed soldiers to capitalize on the confusion of their enemy and led to significant victories in situations that appeared to be certain defeats. Troops who understood tactics and clear communication through training were prepared in the necessary foundations of executing the battle. Troops who knew each other and whose leaders prepared them emotionally and gave orders with the emotional unity in mind ensured the best possible outcome under the circumstances.

Today, a financial institution's revenue model requires continuous readiness both in terms of information availability and the ability to act on it promptly.

REFERENCES

The New York Times.
The Wall Street Journal.
Von Schell, Captain Adolf. *Battle Leadership*, The Marine Corps Assn. (2001).
NASDAQ OMX Historical Stock Prices: www.nasdaq.com
The Federal Reserve Board, FRB: H.15 Release—Selected Interest Rates—Historical Data
    http://www.federalreserve.gov/releases/H15/data.htm

Implementation Issues and the Wide-Reaching Impact on Institutions and the Financial System

CHAPTER 10

Effective Sustainability Management
From Top to Bottom

Contents

> Developing sustainability-management policies, implementing programs, and continuous monitoring of exposure are the key steps towards establishing an effective process to manage tail risk. A PML-based approach provides a sound foundation for these steps.

10.1. KEY PARAMETERS TO DRIVE RISK GOVERNANCE

10.1.1. Two Primary Corporate Objectives

For-profit organizations have two very basic objectives. At the board of directors level, one is often analyzed, reviewed, debated, and stated clearly; the second—though just as important—may be discussed but is rarely analyzed, debated, or stated explicitly because there hasn't been a way to measurably establish it.

The first one—the financial objective—is to capture the full financial potential of the company's business model. To develop this objective, detailed analyses that include industry overviews, competitive reviews, and strength and weakness evaluations are undertaken, and then precise goals are defined and established for return on equity, earnings growth, and profit targets. Each year, at most organizations, a multiyear plan is developed to achieve these goals, and an annual budget is approved.

The second and equally important objective, usually implied but not explicitly stated, is to ensure going-concern sustainability of the company at all times. We will refer to this as the sustainability objective. This objective is often not as well developed, nor as clearly defined, as the financial objective. And frequently it may even be assumed to be a part of the traditional risk-management objective. Because it is often taken for granted, some may argue that boards do have such an objective, which is to always be in business.

Most people would agree that no institution would think about not defining and stating its financial objective and goals clearly. On the other hand, most institutions do not establish a clear sustainability objective and parameters for tail risk, let alone do so in the appropriate hierarchical order. This is the fundamental reason for extreme tail-risk vulnerability at all institutions.

To demonstrate a point about how the sustainability objective needs to be addressed, let's flip this. Imagine for a moment that instead of precisely stating the financial objective and defining measurable earnings or return goals, a company simply states that the financial goal is to always "earn as large a profit as possible." And the annual budget is simply stated as "to make more money than the prior year." What if nothing more is stated because making money is so fundamental to the existence of an institution? Any responsible executive or board member will find such a statement, in lieu of explicitly stated objectives, goals, and policies, to be highly unacceptable, not to mention the fact that without explicit statement of goals, it is nearly impossible to implement effective management and governance. Yet the sustainability objective about maintaining a going-concern is typically stated in such generally vague terms, if stated at all.

In addition, there is another important reason for explicitly stating the sustainability objective and defining and quantifying precise goals. There are two dimensions of risk, as discussed earlier. The parameters of the revenue-driving dimension of risk are established by the financial goals, such as return on equity, profit targets, and limits for earnings volatility. In turn, such financial goals can only be established within the context of the financial objective of the company. Therefore, the revenue-driving dimension of risk can only be managed in the context of the company's financial objective.

The sustainability objective deals with the second—sustainability-related— dimension of risk. However, this sustainability objective is such an imperative that the financial objective can only be meaningful if developed and implemented in the context of ensuring that the institution will always survive. If an institution is not viable and sustainable as a going concern, then the financial objective is irrelevant. To express a financial goal without stating sustainability goals amounts to requiring a certain return from a portfolio without defining any limit on VaR for market risk. Everyone would agree that such an arrangement would be a recipe for disaster. Similarly, for example, a 15% return-on-equity goal without an explicit sustainability goal implies a license to take on whatever tail-risk structure is necessary to deliver the financial goal, which is not what any board intends to do. Therefore, the financial objective can only be defined in the context of a sustainability objective.

10.1.2. Important Hierarchical Relationship

This hierarchical relationship between two primary objectives also establishes a clear hierarchy between the two dimensions of risk, each driven by a distinctly different objective, as shown in Figure 10.1. The sustainability objective establishes goals for tail-risk parameters, or the sustainability-related dimension of risk. This dimension provides the context for the financial objective, which establishes goals for traditional risk-management parameters, or the revenue-driving dimension of risk.

This hierarchical order must be observed to have meaningful, clear, and objective goals and targets. Anything else, or having tail-risk related parameters developed as a part of the traditional risk-management objective, adds subjectivity and amounts to putting the cart before the horse.

Figure 10.1

10.1.3. Sustainability Objective and Goals

Corporate financial objective, goals, and risk-management parameters can only be established meaningfully in the context of the following issues:

- What should be the sustainability objective of the institution?
- What should be the sustainability goals that will drive the sustainability-management process of the institution?

As the governance focus begins at the highest level and moves down the organization hierarchy, other key sustainability-management-related issues must be addressed, such as:

- What size and scope of parameters of extreme exposure are acceptable?
- How much protection should be provided?
- What guidelines should drive programs to protect against extreme tail risk?
- What should be the extreme exposure limit for each business segment?

Addressing such questions and issues leads to tail-risk or sustainability-management policies. To address such issues and develop sound parameters, a measure is required.

10.2. PML AS A MEASURE OF THE EXTREME EXPOSURE PARAMETER

At the core of sustainability management, the two most important questions are:

1. How well are the policies formulated and implemented to prevent the institution from getting too close to the edge, while maximizing its business model potential?
2. How effective are the programs at keeping the institution from going over the edge if it finds itself being pulled too close?

Among the factors impacting how effectively these questions are addressed is how clearly and objectively the parameters of the sustainability-related dimension of risk have been defined and quantified. These parameters drive the sustainability-management process and help develop proactive and effective solutions.

10.2.1. PML Provides Proactive Quantification

The value of using PML as a measure goes beyond quantifying an institution's total extreme exposure. Simply knowing the total PML is neither very useful nor very meaningful for three reasons.

1. PML is not a forecast of what *will* happen. It is a quantification of what *can* happen in the extreme. So simulating the impact of an action on total PML by itself does not say anything about how the institution may weather a crisis. The next crisis may not necessarily be the most extreme, but it may be extreme enough to threaten the going concern.
2. A leveraged financial institution's PML is for the most part so substantial that it is nearly impossible to tackle it in its entirety.
3. An institution cannot eliminate or drastically reduce its total PML or the sustainability gap and still expect to maintain a risk-management-based revenue model.

Yet the real challenge is to manage the PML proactively, and understanding what makes up the total PML is crucial to do so. Gaining a good handle on extreme exposure through PML-based analyses can be leveraged into a number of sustainability-management initiatives. For example:

- Fragmenting total PML into defined actionable components can lead to the formulation of policies, strategies, and limits.
- Analyzing the PML of each portfolio can provide for 3-D discrimination among business segments along the lines of the conceptual illustration in Figure 8.3.
- Internalizing the impact of each component of PML can guide the development of defensive sustainability-enhancement programs akin to BCPs.
- Effective implementation of defensive programs can provide cushions to preserve and extend the protective value of capital.
- Simple and transparent PML analyses, objectively showing strengths and vulnerabilities of the institution in relation to tail risk, can be used for proactive dialogs with external audiences such as regulators and the marketplace.

PML: Only a Supplement, Not a Replacement for Sound Judgment

PML turns abstract extreme exposure into actionable quantification. However, it should not replace sound judgment on limits, targets, and values that must guide risk governance.

The first step in implementing any management process is to define its objective, and then formulate policies and strategies to achieve the objective. Therefore, let's look at an example of how we might fragment the total PML to develop sustainability-management policies.

We will continue with the data from our example used earlier. One can fragment the total PML in a number of ways. One of the ways is by designating the qualitative likelihood of the PML materializing. By adding a dimension of human judgment, we will break down the total PML into three fragments: low-likelihood PML, lower-likelihood PML, and lowest-likelihood PML.

Figure 10.2 depicts a conceptual example of the tail end of the exposure distribution curve, with the severity of loss on the horizontal axis and the probability of the loss on the vertical axis. The vertical axis is shown only for conceptual purposes and is not required to fragment total PML. The illustration shows that our financial institution has a low-likelihood PML of $20 billion; a lower-likelihood PML of $25 billon, to yield a combined low- and lower-likelihood PML of $45 billion; and a lowest-likelihood PML of $35 billion, to give the total low-, lower-, and lowest-likelihood PML of $80 billion mentioned earlier. These translate into a low-likelihood sustainability gap of $5 billion (low-likelihood PML of $20 billion minus capital of $15 billion), a combined low- and lower-likelihood sustainability gap of $30 billion, and the total low-, lower-, and lowest-likelihood sustainability gap of $65 billion.

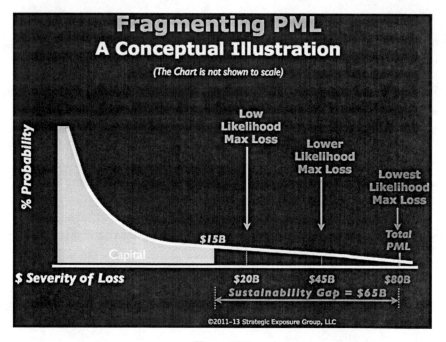

Figure 10.2

Fragmenting the total PML of $80 billion and sustainability gap of $65 billion this way paves the way for a proactive approach. For an institution of the size in our example, it is very difficult, if not impossible, to manage a monolithic $65 billion sustainability gap. By fragmenting it into three smaller fragments, we now have manageable components. The kinds of actions required to manage the first $5 billion gap (with low likelihood) will be quite different from the kinds of actions one might employ to manage the next $25 billion gap (with lower likelihood). For example, there may be some items with relatively higher likelihood of maximum loss than others and, based upon a 3-D discriminatory view of the risk–reward relationship, these may be candidates for elimination to reduce the amount of the low-likelihood gap. There may be other items with lower likelihood of maximum loss that may be better covered by developing disciplined contingency programs than by eliminating them. So there may be a Plan A to address the low-likelihood gap of $5 billion, a Plan B to address the next-lower-likelihood gap of $25 billion, and a Plan C to address the next-lowest-likelihood gap of $35 billion.

PML-based analyses can, therefore, drive several critical initiatives that supplement risk- and capital-management processes and enhance the going-concern sustainability of an institution. Some of these initiatives are summarized ahead.

> **PML: A Discipline to Enhance Risk Governance**
> PML supplements—not replaces—risk management and capital management.

10.3. EFFECTIVE TAIL-RISK OR SUSTAINABILITY MANAGEMENT

10.3.1. Objective Formulation of Policies, Limits, and Guidelines

As mentioned earlier, currently there are no quantitative measures to define tail risk. Therefore, policies, limits, and guidelines are addressed by employing proxies that do not objectively represent the true exposure from extreme tail risk. Such proxies may range from qualitative gut-feel opinions to quantitative measures that may bear little relationship to extreme exposure and often may be an extension of risk-management policies, limits, and guidelines.

A PML-based metric, by focusing on the true exposure from extreme tail risk, enables a quantitative integration of extreme exposure into transparent policy formulation and allows senior managers to exercise judgment to balance sustainability-policy options with revenue and risk-management objectives. Similarly, a PML-based approach optimizes resources by allocating limits among business segments, taking into account the three-dimensional view of the risk–reward relationship.

10.3.2. Implementing Policies, Limits, and Guidelines to Enhance Going-Concern Sustainability

Implementing sound policies and strategies into specific programs enhances the going-concern sustainability of an institution by enabling program decisions based upon objective analyses. For example, implementing a policy that limits the size and characteristics of the sustainability gap through PML-based discrimination will result in a reduction of the tail risk of the institution.

Let us assume that the institution in our example adopts a policy to cap the low–likelihood PML at 10% below the amount of capital. This establishes a goal for managers to reduce low–likelihood extreme exposure by $6.5 billion to $13.5 billion (90% of the capital amount of $15 billion). This policy ensures that the going concern will be maintained through the maximum exposure from the low–likelihood tail risk, as shown in Figure 10.3. In order

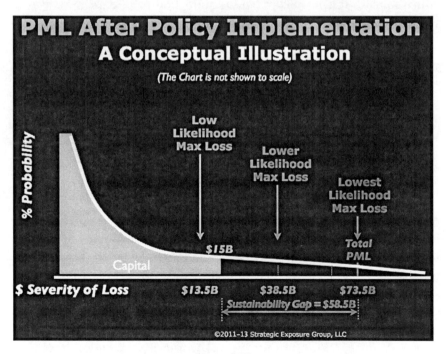

Figure 10.3

to accomplish this goal, managers can target items on the risk-reward matrix as best candidates for restructuring, develop defensive operating programs that reduce the PML, or a combination of both. Effective implementation of such programs will enhance the going-concern sustainability to the tune of at least $5 billion (the reduction in the low-likelihood sustainability gap).

10.3.3. Proactive Continuous Monitoring of Extreme Exposure

An effective process needs more than sound policies and guidelines. It also needs continuous monitoring to ensure there are no unpleasant surprises. This is even more critical today, as progressively more complex revenue models have become more dependent on fast-paced developments in global financial markets. As demonstrated by some of the recent events, complexities of transactions and a lack of a measure make continuous monitoring of extreme exposure opaque and unavailable. Therefore, maintaining transparency through continuous monitoring of a simple metric is imperative.

A PML-based sustainability-management process responds to this critical need via two features. First, it translates complex transactions into a simple measure by responding to complexity with simplicity. Second, because PML is based upon structural factors and not on external conditions, it provides a measure of extreme tail risk at all times regardless of the conditions in the marketplace. Establishing PML-based monitoring of the extreme exposure, therefore, contributes to a significant element of the effective tail-risk-management process.

10.4. EFFECTIVE SUSTAINABILITY MANAGEMENT TO PROTECT CAPITAL

The objective of sustainability management is to preserve and protect capital. So how does sustainability management do this? That's the subject of the next chapter.

Understanding components of total PML leads to the development of effective solutions to manage the tail risk of a financial institution.

CHAPTER 11

Paradoxical Capital Problem

Contents

> The financial industry's need for a bigger cushion to absorb shocks is real. However, simply adding more capital is not an effective solution.

The banking industry has a paradoxical capital problem. There is tremendous pressure to increase the capital base, but it cannot increase capital by adding capital. Let's review this.

Traditionally, financial institutions and regulators address tail risk indirectly through capital adequacy models that suggest a preference for bigger capital cushions to absorb large, unexpected shocks and hits. Therefore, the change in the perception of risk following the experience of 2008 has dramatically increased the intensity of calls for more capital. Actually, such calls are not new. There has always been tension between regulators and bankers about the adequacy of capital. Each crisis simply renews calls for more capital, and the bigger the crisis, the louder the calls.

11.1. THE NEED FOR A BIGGER CUSHION IS REAL BECAUSE OF THE INCREASED PRESSURE ON CAPITAL

Post-2008, based upon regulatory and Basel III developments, several reputable forecasts have projected the industry's global need for additional capital in the hundreds of billons of dollars. The need for a bigger

Managing Extreme Financial Risk

shock-absorbing cushion is real because (i) market risk plays a significantly greater role in a financial institution's revenue model today than it did years ago, and (ii) financial markets around the world have been growing increasingly more volatile, thus changing the risk profile of financial institutions. During the same period, capital needed to absorb shocks from such growing activities has not kept pace with the increase in extreme exposure from market risk.

The net effect has been that while the risk that drives revenue models has changed fundamentally, the approach to dealing with exposure from extreme tail risk has changed only marginally. However, simply looking to increased capital without addressing the factors that drive the need for greater shock-absorbing cushions is neither sustainable nor realistic.

11.2. INCREASED CAPITAL SOLUTIONS ARE NOT SUSTAINABLE

If an institution adds capital, then it needs to generate higher earnings to cover the cost of incremental capital. The quest for higher earnings requires the institution to take on more risk to generate these earnings, as risk management primarily drives the current revenue model. In turn, higher risk creates the need for more capital. This is the paradox: Adding capital actually increases the need for more capital. Therefore, the industry's dependency on increased capital to maintain the current revenue engine is not sustainable.

11.3. INCREASED CAPITAL SOLUTIONS ARE NOT REALISTIC

Given the high cost of capital, it is also questionable if the industry can access the projected huge amount of capital in the near future. Attracting large amounts of capital is difficult in normal times, and may not be realistic given the current and near-term uncertainties and high cost of capital for the financial industry. Recent developments in postponing the implementation of some elements of Basel III may be an indication of this difficulty.

11.4. A NEW APPROACH TO ADDRESSING THE NEED FOR A BIGGER CUSHION IS REQUIRED

Therefore it is clear that something more fundamental must change, as otherwise the financial industry, with its critical role of providing liquidity for the economy, will continue to function under capital constraints rather than operate with a sense of confidence. New solutions are needed if financial institutions are to continue with the risk-management-driven nature of their revenue models.

11.5. SUSTAINABILITY MANAGEMENT OFFERS A NEW SOLUTION BY ALLEVIATING THE PRESSURE ON CAPITAL

This is where sustainability management comes in. Sustainability management does not add capital. However, managing tail risk effectively—by preserving and protecting capital from unexpected losses—can make capital go further.

There are two options to enhance sustainability via capital: the supply option and the demand option. The current approach of focusing only on the supply side—i.e., *increasing* capital—for the reasons outlined earlier does not seem like a very good option. The other approach—focused on reducing demand on capital—can make the current stock of capital go farther through well-structured defensive programs that *preserve and protect capital*. There is another significant reason for focusing on the demand option to enhance the sustainability of an institution.

11.6. ANOTHER REASON FOR A NEW APPROACH

In the banking industry, capital needs are currently driven by regulatory requirements, which are designed to meet certain regulatory objectives. As discussed earlier, regulatory objectives, while they may encourage maintaining going-concerns, primarily relate to the preservation of the financial system, prevention of systemic problems, and minimizing taxpayer costs. On the other hand, going-concern objectives must address the ongoing integrity of an institution. There is a significant gap between these objectives, with implications for the going-concern sustainability management of an institution.

Regulatory objectives can be met without necessary regard for the going-concern integrity of an institution, as shown by the experiences of Bear Stearns, Washington Mutual, and Wachovia, even though this is not how regulators would like to pursue their objective. In each institution's case, the regulatory objective was achieved even though the loss of going-concern integrity resulted in the loss of most, if not all, of the shareholder value.

Understandably from a regulatory perspective, going-concern integrity is a lower priority than preserving the financial system. Because the regulatory objective can be met without maintaining going-concern integrity, it implies that the threshold for maintaining going-concern integrity is higher than the one needed to meet regulatory objectives. Because of this threshold gap, regulatory objectives don't go far enough to address the going-concern integrity of financial institutions.

The Basel framework, or another similar approach, drives the current capital requirement debate. Such frameworks of capital requirement are vast and complex. Also understandably, because of the high cost of capital, the industry's capital requirement debate is pretty intense. In the heat of this debate, focused on the complex framework, something as simple as the fact that meeting the regulatory capital requirement is no assurance of survival is often forgotten. In August 2012, Andrew Haldane and Vasileios Madouros of Bank of England presented the results of one of their bank capital analyses at a Federal Reserve Bank conference. Their presentation included several charts. "Chart 3 plots the Basel risk-based capital ratios for the sample of global banks on an ascending scale, distinguishing 'failed' and 'surviving' banks. There is little visual correlation between levels of regulatory capital and subsequent bank failure. That is confirmed in Chart 4, which … compares levels of risk-based capital in failed and surviving banks. These are not statistically significantly different."[1]

Thus the current regulatory capital requirements—with systemic preservation in mind—can be met without necessarily having the assurance of adequate capital to maintain the going-concern integrity of a financial institution. This implies that the capital needed to maintain the integrity of a going concern is higher than the regulatory requirement.

If institutions have a hard time fulfilling the regulatory capital requirement currently, then it is nearly impossible to address the higher going-concern capital requirement through the supply option only. Therefore, the demand option must be the primary focus of enhancing sustainability in lieu of the supply-option approach to capital.

11.7. A CHANGE IS NEEDED IN HOW CAPITAL IS DEPLOYED

Focusing on the demand option to enhance sustainability requires turning the institutional capital into the last defense against shocks and hits. This represents a fundamental change from the current practice of employing

---

[1] Haldane and Madouros (2012)

capital as the first and the only defense against shocks and hits. This is a critical point in relation to sustainability management. What does it mean and what are its implications? Let's discuss this in the next chapter.

A new approach to capital management is needed.

REFERENCES

Basel Committee on Banking Supervision, 2010. Basel III: A global regulatory framework for more resilient banks and banking systems. Available at: http://www.bis.org/publ/bcbs189_dec2010.htm.

Haldane, Andrew, Madouros, Vasileios, 2012. *The Dog and The Frisbee*. Presented at the Federal Reserve Bank of Kansas City's 36th economic policy symposium: "The Changing Policy Landscape" at Jackson Hole, WY, Available at: www.bankofengland.co.uk/publications/Pages/speeches/default.aspx.

CHAPTER 12

Capital as the Last Defense vs the First Defense

Contents

> Effective sustainability-enhancement programs blunt the impact of shocks and hits, and thus extend the protective value of the capital.

The difference between capital as the first and the only defense versus the last defense may sound subtle, but it has far-reaching implications for capital adequacy as well as for revenue models.

The financial industry is the only major industry that employs capital as the first and the only tangible defense against exposure from risk. Some may argue with this statement. In the banking industry it is often mentioned that quality of earnings, quality of management, effectiveness of the management process, etc. are the first defenses against losses, which is true. However, these are all intangibles, and they do not provide the same measurable and objective protection as well-defined tangible programs do. For example, no risk-management professional would recommend, nor senior managers would accept, an intangible like the quality of personnel/managers as a portfolio hedge instead of explicit tangible programs that define limits and controls. So why should capital protection programs be dependent on intangibles? Such intangibles are sound practices to protect capital, and they should be encouraged, but they are not a substitute for tangible defenses, thus leaving the capital as the first and only tangible defense against risk.

Objective of Sustainability Management:
To preserve and protect capital from risk.

Because of the high cost, no other industry would think of using capital as the primary source of protection against losses from risk. Most industries go out of their way to develop, implement, and monitor specific risk-management and other sustainability-management programs to ensure that such programs meet their objective to protect capital. For example, as depicted in Figure 12.1, nonfinancial companies provide elaborate sustainability programs in addition to operating programs to protect capital against exposure from one of the largest risks of a major business interruption. The protective value of such programs is indicated by the fact that insurance companies, the last defense in front of capital, offer premium discounts for business interruption insurance if these protective programs are effectively implemented. The net effect of these programs is to provide first defense against unexpected losses and turn the entity's capital into the last defense against exposure from risk. Such programs have costs, and when triggered to provide protection they may also involve large expenses, but these costs are far less than the cost of the alternative: to use capital as a first defense.

Figure 12.1

12.1. MORE AND STRONGER DEFENSES MEAN LESS PRESSURE ON CAPITAL

Identifying and quantifying the components that contribute to total PML can enable the development of specific sustainability-enhancement programs that, when implemented in a disciplined, credible manner, can provide the first tangible defense against unexpected losses, reduce the demand on capital, and thus protect the capital.

Each institution must balance the needs to drive the revenue engine to its full potential and to maintain going-concern sustainability through extreme crises. Therefore, in order to allow risk to continue to drive the revenue engine in normal times—which is most of the time—and yet protect the institution from tail risk, sustainability-enhancement programs can be developed and implemented as contingency programs. This allows an institution to capture the full potential of the revenue model aggressively and prudently.

12.2. SUSTAINABILITY-ENHANCEMENT PROGRAMS

Everyone knows that the time to plan and install smoke detectors, fire sprinklers, and other defensive programs is not when the building is on fire, but well ahead of time. Similarly, the way to deal with capital defenses and protective programs to sustain a going concern is well before an extreme financial crisis. Such programs, akin to smoke detectors, fire sprinklers, and BCPs, are best planned and implemented as contingency programs, which get triggered with predefined criteria. The concept is not new; only its focus and how it may be applied is new.

From time to time, one hears of plans (generally because of regulatory pressure) to supplement capital. Some plans call for balance sheet restructuring; others call for asset sales to beef up the institutional capital by converting unrecorded gains into equity. Such programs are planned and implemented after capital has already taken a hit. Even if planning for such actions were to be completed ahead of time, because of the fast-paced marketplace, an institution in a crisis does not have the luxury of waiting weeks and months to implement them. Any counteraction needs to be quick and effective. The key difference between actions to convert unrecorded gains into equity and defensive sustainability-enhancement programs is that effective sustainability management requires implementation as a first defense rather than a response after the capital has been depleted. Another significant difference is that after-the-hit programs generally involve sale of assets outside the operating functions, with little or no impact on PMLs. Proactive sustainability management requires taking action in relation to operating assets and other items to reduce PML before the crisis to blunt the impact of unexpected losses on capital. Despite the disadvantages stated here, after-the-hit programs should continue to be a part of corporate plans, but not be primarily relied upon for effective sustainability management.

Similar to the BCP's role in relation to business continuity management, sustainability-enhancement contingency programs are one of the most important parts of a sustainability-management process. This is the frontline of the battle in a crisis and the outcome of these programs could determine the going-concern sustainability of the institution. The effectiveness of sustainability-enhancement contingency programs depends to a great degree upon how well and carefully certain critical issues, such as those listed below, have been addressed upfront.

- What should be the objective and scope of sustainability-enhancement contingency programs?
- How much protection should be provided?
- How far is an organization willing to go in a financial crisis to maintain going-concern sustainability?
- How much cost can be justified in developing, implementing, and maintaining sustainability-enhancement contingency programs, and how much when they are triggered?
- When should they be triggered? What should be the mechanism to trigger them?
- How do you ensure, on an ongoing basis, that they can be counted upon to (i) trigger when they should, and (ii) reliably meet the stated objective and scope?

While such issues require the collective wisdom of the senior-most management team, these judgments need to be based upon objective and clearly defined information. PML-based analyses, with a detailed description of the components of the total extreme exposure, provide a solid foundation for addressing such critical issues.

The outcome of sustainability-enhancement contingency programs does not provide additional capital. Such programs cannot substitute if an institution needs capital. However, capital planning and adequacy models should consider how such programs could effectively blunt the impact of unexpected shocks.

Sustainability-enhancement contingency programs, similar to BCPs, require upfront investments, and when triggered they will have significant costs and impact on the institution's asset portfolio. While they are not capital in a financial sense, their effectiveness is tantamount to having capital. For example, if there were effective programs to reduce PML by $5 billion, then these programs provide the same protection as having $5 billion in additional capital without raising any capital. Therefore, because of their impact on preserving and protecting capital, they are the equivalent of the cheapest form of capital. Furthermore, developing and implementing effective shock-absorbing cushions, such as contingency programs, is a more effective way to relieve the pressure on capital, and far cheaper than adding capital to absorb shocks in an extreme crisis.

Three Critical Requirements of Contingency Programs:
- Clearly established triggers
- Effectiveness not dependent upon external factors
- Timely implementation

As discussed earlier, the capital adequacy discussion for financial institutions centers on regulatory objectives. Earlier we talked about a gap between regulatory objectives and institutional interests in relation to the sustainability of an institution. How wide is this gap? Can there be a convergence of these objectives and interests? Let's discuss this in the next couple of chapters.

Implementing effective sustainability-enhancement programs is tantamount to adding capital to maintain the going-concern sustainability at a far lower cost.

CHAPTER 13

Tail Risk, Regulatory Supervision, and Systemic Risk
Missing Links

Contents

> There appears to be a conflict between regulatory objectives and institutional interests. Or is it more of a disconnect because of a missing link?

The relationship between regulators and financial institutions can be described in many ways, but most people would probably not call them allies. While the relationship is not totally antagonistic, it is also not like partners working towards common goals. Some tension is expected because of the supervisory role of regulators, which often requires drawing boundaries and limits. Regulators view such boundaries and limits as necessary to fulfill their mandate.

From the other side, financial institutions view regulations-defining such boundaries and limits-as restrictive, often unnecessarily or overly so. These boundaries and limits must be complied with, not because institutions perceive them to add value to their businesses, but because this is the requirement if an institution wants to be in this business. This apparent divergence of institutional interests and regulatory requirements gives rise to conflicts.

13.1. REGULATORY OBJECTIVES

Most financial industry regulators have an objective to protect the financial system and minimize taxpayer costs in case of a needed action by the government. Therefore, regulators protect financial institutions not because

99

they empathize with investors, but because this is how they achieve their own objective. However, how this is done often creates conflicts.

In relation to extreme financial risks, until recently, regulators have been monitoring financial institutions by peering through the prism of traditional risk management. In fact, Basel II regulations even allowed financial institutions to derive their capital requirements by using the same risk management models that are used to drive the institution's revenue engine.[1] The crisis of 2008 highlighted a couple of problems with this approach.

First, as discussed previously, information and analyses related to traditional risk management are designed to structure, preserve, and protect profits from risk. All risk management models are geared towards that goal. Obviously, preserving and protecting profits is important, but maintaining a going concern or protecting the financial system goes far beyond preserving and protecting profits. In this regard, these models and their information fall significantly short of preserving and protecting a going concern.

Secondly, traditional risk-management models are driven by historical data. Therefore, employing these models to prepare for extreme tail-risk events and then managing an actual extreme crisis is analogous to planning a driving trip based upon where one has come from and steering the vehicle through a storm by looking in the rear-view mirror. Risk-management models have a limited, useful role in relation to the management of tail risk, but that role is in the context of a sustainability-management framework, not as the primary tool for this purpose.

There are two consequences of monitoring extreme financial risks through the prism of traditional risk management.

1. There is the potential to miss out on critical exposure from extreme tail risk, as shown by some of the events over the last five years.

2. Because of the regulators' search for vulnerabilities by looking through the prism of what drives the revenue engine, there is a sense of second guessing and alienation between regulators and institutions that can border on hostility. How often one hears that regulators "don't really understand what we are trying to do!" Actually, regulators don't need to understand the profit end of these models and transactions, as their quest is for what can go wrong and jeopardize the institution and how well the institution is prepared to manage and deal with such adversity. This sows the seeds of the conflict.

---

[1] Basel Committee on Banking Supervision (1996) (2004)

After the experience of the last financial crisis, regulators have developed some of their own mechanisms, such as stress-testing models, where their own assumptions are run through a black box to simulate the impact of an extreme situation. Stress testing is a step in the right direction because it focuses on extreme situations. However, this has three critical problems.

1. As discussed previously, stress testing employs subjective assumptions and scenarios to simulate shocks to an institution. Such scenarios may seem quite stressful compared to normal circumstances, but they are definitely not representative of the most extreme events. The fact is, as every crisis (including the one in 2008) shows, no one can be certain of what extreme events an institution may face. All institutional crises are a failure of preparedness due to lack of anticipation. Therefore, the use of subjective assumptions and scenarios may not fully identify and necessarily protect against all vulnerabilities.

2. It is natural to expect institutions that are impacted by the results of stress testing to try to figure out what drives the regulatory black box, which they will do sooner or later. As more and more institutions do, they may try to position and run their businesses to score better on the regulatory testing. This may actually create a new element of institutional and systemic risk due to the potential to concentrate risk among institutions that try to find ways to score better on the regulatory scorecard. (For further details, please see the appendix for a recent WSJ article: *"The Fed's Stress Tests Add Risk to the Financial System,"* by Til Schuermann of Oliver Wyman, Inc., and former senior vice president at the Federal Reserve Bank of New York.)

3. Because of its opacity, stress testing cannot be employed as a managerial tool at financial institutions, making it difficult to formulate policies to drive the managerial process with a defined goal in mind.

All responsible parties would agree that some regulatory boundaries and limits are appropriately needed. The crisis of 2008 highlighted the problems with the rear-view approach. But it remains to be seen if the subjective approach of stress testing is the right way to derive and implement boundaries and limits effectively to nurture a healthy industry.

13.2. INSTITUTIONAL RESPONSE

It is well known that the industry views regulatory requirements as a restrictive mandate that financial institutions must live with. Over the years, particularly since 2008, regulatory requirements have become progressively more complex to understand and harder to see how they relate to a better and healthier industry. Given human nature, it is understandable why people treat government requirements as a bureaucratic exercise if they can't perceive any benefit from the mandate. So in the absence of any internalized benefits, this often leads to incentive to create ways around the restrictive mandate, while appearing to meet the regulatory requirements. Such reactions often result in new and generally more complex ways to pursue the institutional agenda around the regulatory restrictions. This actually increases risk by adding complexities and often keeps regulatory objectives from being optimally achieved.

For this reason, stress testing and other similar regulatory monitoring mechanisms become a parallel bureaucratic system rather than an internalized mechanism that adds value to institutions other than to satisfy regulatory requirements.

Therefore, pursued in this manner, a conflict is perceived between regulatory requirements and institutional interests.

13.3. RECONCILING OBJECTIVES

If regulators achieve their objectives by protecting institutions through regulations, then why is it that institutions do not see such regulations as beneficial?

This is because while institutions have an implicit objective to protect themselves by maintaining sustainability, there is a disconnect. There are very few, if any, explicit, objective, and transparent links between an implicit sustainability objective and an institution's operations. Everyday business is run to capture the full potential of the business model within stated policies, limits, and guidelines that often do not have an explicit link to the implicit sustainability objective.

Regulators look at the same operations and conclude—sometimes subjectively—that some of them are not in the best interest of the institutions, whereas the institutions may look at them and conclude them to be important to achieve their profit goals.

Hence, the conflict is born because the operations are viewed from two apparently different perspectives, even though both parties have a common interest to protect the sustainability of the institution. It is important to address and resolve this conflict in order for the regulatory-institutional relationship to be productive.

That will happen only if institutional interests and regulatory objectives converge towards a common approach. So how do you achieve this convergence? This is the subject of the next chapter.

Many of the recent regulatory developments, including stress testing, represent a step in the right direction. However, they do not help bring about the convergence of regulatory and institution objectives. Such a convergence can get both sides to focus on the same objective and thus both enhance sustainability and reduce systemic risk by its effective implementation.

REFERENCES

Basel Committee on Banking Supervision, 1996. Basel III: Overview of the amendments to the capital accord to incorporate market risks. Available at: http://www.bis.org/publ/bcbs23.pdf.

Basel Committee on Banking Supervision, 2004. International Convergence of Capital Measurement and Capital Standards: a Revised Framework. Available at: http://www.bis.org/publ/bcbs107.pdf.

Schuermann, Til, 2013. *The Fed's Stress Tests Add Risk to the Financial System.* The Wall Street Journal, March 19, 2013.

CHAPTER 14

Convergence of Regulatory Objectives and Institutional Interests
Alignment of Goals to Enhance Sustainability and Reduce Systemic Risk

Contents

> There is significant common ground between institutions and regulators. An explicit focus on sustainability management can turn this common ground into a convergence of interests.

On the surface, it may be easy to conclude that there is a conflict, and the pursuit of institutional interests beyond some undefined boundary is at odds with regulatory objectives. A regulatory attempt to draw such a boundary is often opposed vigorously by the industry, as seen recently in relation to the Volcker rule.

14.1. APPARENT CONFLICT

Regulators maintain their supervisory role through reviews and monitoring of operations and performance of institutions. They do so by looking at each institution and its *modus operandi*. This includes a review of its business model, plans, policies, governance and management of risks, client and customer base, financial and analytical models, financial statements, audit reports, etc., as well as an assessment of intangibles, such as management experience and strength, managerial and decision-making processes, reporting and controls, marketplace reputation, etc. In other words, they use objective observations and subjective assessment of many tangible and intangible factors that may have a bearing on an institution's going-concern sustainability. In the end regulators turn this review, as well as output from their black box, into opinions about the institution's strengths, vulnerabilities, and likelihood to sustain a going concern in extreme events.

Despite extensive analyses, because they do not include objective and transparent input about extreme tail risk, such reviews often result in opinions that are viewed by institutions as subjective. Institutions may look at the same variables and draw conclusions that may be at odds with the regulatory view. This often gives rise to a disagreement, particularly if key opinions are not favorable to the institution, which starts a chain of arguments that create the conflict.

14.2. THE CHALLENGE

As discussed earlier, institutions today do not have an explicit focus on going-concern sustainability management, making it difficult if not impossible to gauge objectively how an institution may fare in an extreme situation.

Now imagine an institution that prides itself on effective sustainability management.

- Its board has an explicit statement of sustainability objective, with defined quantitative targets and limits.
- It has clearly formulated sustainability corporate policies to provide guidance to the management of the institution.
- It has a distinct management process to proactively address the going-concern sustainability of the institution, with all senior managers well versed in sustainability management issues.
- It has PML limits assigned to each of its business segments, who in turn have implemented a mechanism to assign similar limits to all of their portfolios and to discriminate among transactions using a complete 3-D view of the risk-reward relationship.
- As a part of the managerial process, it has strong control mechanisms to report, monitor, and manage limits.
- Each of its business segments has specific credible plans and programs with clearly pre-defined triggers, coordinated through corporate criteria, to protect the institutional capital in the event of a crisis. The readiness of these plans is documented and tested regularly.

- Each senior manager's performance evaluation metrics includes at least one meaningful sustainability-management goal.
- In other words, it has a sustainability-management process that qualifies as outstanding.

14.3. CONVERGENCE TOWARDS COMMON GOALS

In this scenario, the focus of regulatory review would be quite different from the current approach. Regulators would still review all the items and factors they have been monitoring, but their primary focus will be on critical issues, such as the following.

- Is the corporate objective clearly stated to indicate the institution's going-concern-sustainability priority? Is it a prudent and realistic objective? Is the objective and goal-setting exercise backed up by sound analyses? Is there a mechanism to report PML exposure from major business segments?
- Are business segment limits reasonably developed, with objective tradeoffs between financial return, risk-management measures, and PML measures?
- Are there sound policies that establish management's approach to PML and sustainability exposure throughout the organization? Have they been communicated clearly?
- Are there sound governance guidelines that encourage risk taking consistent with the institution's financial and sustainability objectives?
- Do individuals in key management roles have a good understanding of what it takes to supervise and ensure adherence to sustainability management policies and balance risk-reward tradeoff by using the 3-D matrix?
- Is the audit committee of the board fully engaged in reviewing reports and ensuring proper governance that includes sustainability management?

These are all proactive steps that an institution can and should implement to add shareholder value. It so happens that these steps also advance the regulatory objective of protecting the institution and, thus, the financial system. Therefore, the primary regulatory focus will shift from understanding the risks in what institutions are doing to achieve their profits goals to evaluating how effective is the sustainability-management process.

A review specifically focused on such issues will give regulators a much more objective basis for addressing going-concern issues with the senior management and the board than a subjective view of selected transactions. Under this scenario if there is a disagreement, it is about a specific item that points out a weakness, rather than regulatory objections to certain transactions for reasons that may appear to be arbitrary and subjective opinions. For example, under this scenario, the issue in relation to the Volcker rule is not whether the activity in question is or is not in the best interest of institutions, but rather how does an institution justify the resulting extreme exposures in relation to sound institutional objectives and policies driving sustainability management.

Such a regulatory review, focused on the institution's sustainability management process, will also help the board of an institution obtain an independent perspective on its effectiveness.

This will lead to a convergence of objectives and interests, providing right incentives to the managers of financial institutions.

14.4. REDUCTION OF SYSTEMIC RISK

As discussed earlier, the institutional threshold for going-concern sustainability is higher than the regulatory threshold for protecting the financial system. In addition, effective sustainability management programs enhance the going-concern integrity of an institution. Therefore, an effective sustainability management process at each institution actually reduces systemic risk and the need for regulatory intervention in a crisis to protect the system. Because of sound and credible sustainability management programs, it creates a bigger cushion in front of an institution's capital, reducing the amount of assistance needed in case of regulatory intervention in a crisis. This will advance public interest significantly.

Along the same lines, can effective sustainability management—along with the use of a PML-based approach to communicate with stakeholders—reduce marketplace anxiety and thus add further shareholder value?

An effective sustainability management process can turn the sometimes adversarial relationship between regulators and financial institutions into a productive and effective partnership that adds shareholder value and reduces systemic risk.

Telling Your Story Effectively to Alleviate Marketplace Anxiety

Contents

15.1. High Level of Anxiety   109
    15.1.1. Too Big to Fail! Too Big to Understand! Too Big to Exist!   109
    15.1.2. More Disclosure, More Restrictions, and More Regulations
        Are Demanded   110
    15.1.3. Stress Testing and Basel III Have Helped Shore Up Confidence
        And Reduce Some Anxiety   110
15.2. A New Approach to Communicating Tail Risk Is Needed   111
15.3. Reducing Anxiety, Building Greater Confidence, and Adding
    Shareholder Value   111
15.4. Objective Public Policy Debate   112
15.5. Too Complex to Manage?   112

> Five years after the last crisis, a high level of anxiety persists, as the marketplace doesn't have a way to gauge a financial institution's ability to navigate and survive the next crisis.

15.1. HIGH LEVEL OF ANXIETY

15.1.1. Too Big to Fail! Too Big to Understand! Too Big to Exist!

Since the crisis of 2008–2009, risk has created a high level of anxiety among all parties with an interest in the financial industry. This includes regulators, politicians, investors, consumers, corporations, and even the management of financial institutions. This is because revenue models and related risks are too complex to understand easily, making it nearly impossible for the market to gauge the strength and vulnerabilities of financial institutions given the possibility of another extreme financial crisis.

New laws have been enacted. New regulations have been added. Large amounts of resources have been invested in new analytics, systems, processes, and controls. While several of these developments have ensured that some of the flagrant experiences that led to the 2008 crisis will not happen again, there is no simple, objective, and transparent way to gauge a

Managing Extreme Financial Risk

© 2014 Elsevier Inc.
All rights reserved.

financial institution's ability to survive another crisis. New laws and regulations, while intended to avoid the systemic experience of 2008, have added confusion and complexity. No one can say with confidence that the fundamental problem tail-risk management has been addressed.

15.1.2. More Disclosure, More Restrictions, and More Regulations Are Demanded

Every week there are demands for some new action to avoid the problems experienced in the last crisis. Unfortunately, none of the solutions often mentioned or implemented to date will by themselves reduce the anxiety, as none communicates nor addresses objectively how strong or weak an institution is and how likely it is to survive a sudden financial crisis or exposure from extreme tail risk. This requires more than just additional disclosure or regulations. For example, more disclosure alone, without an objective, transparent, and easy-to-understand context of sustainability of an institution, will only make matters worse. Without addressing the underlying issues, more new disclosure will add to the confusion, which will call for additional disclosure, and thus further heighten the anxiety.

15.1.3. Stress Testing and Basel III Have Helped Shore Up Confidence And Reduce Some Anxiety

While stress testing and Basel III have helped somewhat, they have also highlighted areas of needed improvements. Stress testing, while a step in the right direction, can benefit significantly if a couple of issues can be addressed. Currently, it lacks transparency. It provides a pass/fail verdict based upon a black-box review, without enabling the marketplace to easily understand an institution's vulnerability, strength, or likelihood to survive a sudden financial crisis. This is fine as a first major step after the 2008 crisis, but it needs to be supplemented.

Second, as discussed previously, stress testing relies on subjective scenarios and assumptions. If the next crisis were to be just like the previous one or along the lines of the assumptions, the stress testing may change the outcome if actions have been taken to correct vulnerabilities. However, experience shows that no two crises are alike. If the next crisis is sparked by a combination of factors different from the ones that contributed to previous ones, then the assumptions underlying stress testing may not be very helpful. Several recent events since 2008 demonstrate the need to address this issue.

Therefore, the results of stress testing—while providing some assurances—have significant limitations in relation to addressing marketplace anxiety.

15.2. A NEW APPROACH TO COMMUNICATING TAIL RISK IS NEEDED

Every financial institution is facing pressure to show that significant progress has been made since 2008. Today, when inquiring about an institution's resiliency and ability to withstand and survive another crisis, one often hears:

It can't happen to us. We are well-diversified.

Our equity ratio exceeds the regulatory requirements.

We are ahead of the Basel III implementation requirements.

We passed the stress test.

We have implemented the new living will provision.

We have a fortress balance sheet.

Are these self-serving statements? Do they represent a false sense of security? Or are they really true this time as compared to the similar claims in the pre-2008 era? Can they be backed by an objective review of the issues that impact an institution's ability to handle exposure from extreme tail risk? How does one demonstrate the validity of these statements objectively, simply, and transparently?

Actually, even though all of them may be true, none of these statements captures an institution's going-concern strength in the face of a sudden financial crisis. For example, a statement such as *"our equity ratio of x% is higher than the regulatory requirement of y%"* is factually correct, but it is not an indicator of an institution's strength in relation to its going-concern sustainability. Meeting a particular equity ratio is no assurance of survival in an extreme crisis. Similarly, there are no transparent, objective, and demonstrated links between various steps taken by institutions since 2008 and an enhancement in going-concern sustainability. Nor is there an objective way to gauge the relative effectiveness of various initiatives.

Therefore, a new approach is needed to simply, objectively, and transparently communicate tail-risk management strength to the marketplace.

15.3. REDUCING ANXIETY, BUILDING GREATER CONFIDENCE, AND ADDING SHAREHOLDER VALUE

This is the power of the PML-based approach! Since there are no black boxes or subjective assumptions, a PML-based sustainability management analysis can quantify the real exposure and show how an initiative is mitigating it or how the institution is managing it to ensure survival through a sudden financial crisis. For example, the impregnability of a fortress balance sheet can be demonstrated more effectively using an easy-to-understand and transparent PML-based analysis than through subjective anecdotal ratios or claims.

A transparent and simple dialog—using a PML-based sustainability/tail-risk analysis—will help investors expand their understanding of not just how the institution's revenue model works, but also how it will fare through another crisis. Such an understanding will enable investors to discriminate between institutions, and thus (i) reduce the overall anxiety in the marketplace, and (ii) reward the institutions that have a superior handle on tail risk. Therefore, getting investors to understand the institution's story better will reduce anxiety, build greater confidence, and add shareholder value.

15.4. OBJECTIVE PUBLIC POLICY DEBATE

Five years after the last financial crisis, public debate continues on several issues, including the need for additional regulations and demands to break up large institutions to reduce systemic risk. This debate also lacks an objective foundation and knowledge about financial institutions' strength or vulnerabilities and ability to survive another crisis. References are often made to anecdotal ratios or to developments that have very little or no bearing on the sustainability of an institution; these only add confusion to the debate. Therefore, by enabling a transparent discussion, a focus on extreme tail risk and going-concern sustainability can advance the too-big-to-fail public policy debate of the last five years more objectively.

15.5. TOO COMPLEX TO MANAGE?

There is a general sentiment often mentioned that today's large financial institutions are too complex for anyone to comprehend and manage. Despite the complexities, they must be managed effectively. Based upon the experience of 2008, are there certain factors that need emphasizing in relation to the complexity and financial crises?

> A PML-based approach can help communicate the story more effectively and thus reduce anxiety, add market discipline into ensuring going-concern sustainability, and advance the public policy debate.

CHAPTER 16

Critical Factors in Preparing for an Extreme Financial Crisis

A former senior executive who wishes to remain anonymous

Contents

> The crisis of 2008 was different from any other crisis of the last 70 years because of the scope of its depth and breadth. Importantly, its depth and breadth resulted from the unprecedented concentration of exposure from tail risk that was missed for many reasons. It is startling to realize how basic some of these reasons were.

16.1. AIG TIMELINE

As I am sitting in my office overlooking midtown Manhattan, it is hard to believe that the week started only 11 hours ago. It already seems like the longest week ever. At a meeting barely three hours ago, everyone seemed stunned by how much the financial world has changed since last Friday, September 12, 2008. Staring out of the window, I am reflecting on and trying to absorb specific events related to AIG.

The downgrade this evening from AA to A- prompted a collateral call for a staggering amount of $14.5 billion. Since the Lehman Brothers bankruptcy this morning, no one could be sure of what is to come next. The subsequent panic has frozen the market; because of a lack of buyers, it is not clear where the market prices of assets are.

About two weeks ago, we reviewed and discussed AIG's credit. At that time, AIG seemed well capitalized, with significant global assets. There was some concern about the lack of complete transparency of AIG's exposure to other counterparties, including the number of parties involved. But on that day, any concern about AIG almost seemed to be a side issue. The attention was focused more on the liquidity positions at major investment banks like Morgan Stanley, Goldman Sachs, Lehman Brothers, and Merrill Lynch. As I am thinking about that discussion, my mind wanders off to a series of events that began almost 18 months ago.

First Quarter 2007, As I was waiting in the executive suite of AIG, I remember thinking, "this is a very different company today" as I reviewed the metamorphosis of AIG in my mind. I couldn't help but think about the AIG I had known. Hank Greenberg, who had been gone only 24 months, ran an autocratic organization. He knew about all the subsidiary companies, was involved in managing their risks, and took a hands-on approach to balancing the overall exposure of AIG's balance sheet. His departure, coupled with the settlement with the New York Attorney General's office, prompted all three rating agencies to cut AIG's credit rating from AAA to AA.

A few minutes later, I found myself being introduced to the current CEO, Martin Sullivan. My meeting with him and the company treasurer Bob Gender was very useful, as my positive assessment was reinforced. The company was well capitalized. There was a tremendous amount of experience in all forms of insurance products and a very strong culture of sales and marketing because of CEO Sullivan's successful experience. An entrepreneurial atmosphere permeated the company's four major business segments. The AIG Financial Products (AIGFP) business was growing and contributing major profits to corporate earnings. It was a leader in structured swaps and credit default swap (CDS) transactions. Because of the large transaction volume, AIG was a significant counterparty to most of the global financial institutions. One of the biggest corporate challenges at this point seemed to be cash management, as the company was flush with liquidity.

The only unknown I remember related to the CEO's and treasurer's experience with complex financial securities, particularly as related to their valuations and risks. Even though it was eclipsed by all the positive reinforcements, it was hard to miss the explosive growth in AIGFP's book on insurance for financial products like credit default swaps, collateralized debt obligations (CDOs), and residential and commercial mortgage-backed securities. Because of AIG's AA rating, there was no need to post collaterals to back up these transactions. Therefore, cash flow from the sale of these financial insurance products was a very strong one-way tide that seemed to be turning into a bigger surge everyday.

What could be better! Writing insurance for these financial products raked in huge profits, with no significant capital allocations, and no cash calls to post collateral. All the securities, regardless of their fair-market value designation of level 1, 2, or 3, were listed at par, and many were rated AAA by rating agencies. It was what any business would like to have!

September 2007, AIG reported a staggering $352 million loss in CDS in the financial products business.

This caused a rush of adrenaline at our institution as loan agreements were pulled out for review. Our institution's exposure to AIG ran into billions through *direct loans, CDS protection purchased from AIG, and other "CDS wrapped" trans-actions. A downgrade would trigger a huge collateral call on AIG. The numbers were quite sobering. But I remember the general sentiment: "Hey, this is AIG!" The net assessment was that the downgrade was highly unlikely. AIG had just raised $20 billion through a series of capital transactions. Their shareholders' equity stood at over $78 billion, with total consolidated assets of over $1 trillion as of June 30, 2008.*

In addition, a review of traditional risk-management indicators suggested ample capital, cash, and securities to cover any collateral call that AIG may face in a hypo-thetically extreme scenario. The concern about the lack of transparency had grown significantly as the question kept coming up: "How much counterparty exposure to how many parties?" But discussions always concluded that AIG had sufficient resources to cover its obligations.

June 15, 2008, Just weeks after J.P. Morgan Chase had completed the acquisition of Bear Stearns, AIG reported a shocking $5.6 billion loss attributable to AIGFP's CDS portfolio, along with $20 billion in write-downs on CDS guarantees and an addi-tional $18 billion write-down on mortgage- and asset-backed securities during the previous three quarters.

Martin Sullivan was replaced with a new CEO, Bob Willumstad, an experienced Citi-group banker and facilitator of Citi's merger with Travelers. However, his experience in leading a large global institution with complex financial securities, their valua-tion, and risks was untested.

September 15, 2008, There was a full-blown panic at our institution as rumors began swirling around this morning. If Lehman wasn't rescued, who could be next? Who will come to AIG's rescue? What happens if there is no rescue? Will we survive our exposure to AIG? How much exposure?

16.2. KEY OBSERVATIONS

The timeline just summarized is a 50,000-foot view of selected events as they snowballed into an out-of-control train speeding towards a wreck. It has also been greatly simplified, to pick just a few statistics with the advantage of hindsight.

This timeline doesn't reveal anything not known before. One could write a 1,000-page book and still not cover all the details of the AIG experience. So in putting this timeline together, I focused on three key points in relation to today's financial institution's ability to deal with potential extreme financial crises. Each of these points is obvious common sense, but each needs stating for emphasis as organizations often overlook them.

- Sound human judgment at the highest level is the most important factor despite— or because of—the complexity.
- Readiness is critical. AIG was highly unprepared, and turning to an untested leader with untested ability to deal with the complexity in the middle of a crisis added to the unpreparedness.
- Control is critical, and it comes from simplicity to always know easily and objectively complex things that can seriously damage the institution.

16.3. SOUND HUMAN JUDGMENT, NOT ROCKET SCIENCE

At first glance, today's financial institutions seem too complex to manage. And they are getting more complex every day in their continuing quest to explore new frontiers and incorporating disciplines one didn't know existed to find that extra return from hard-to-understand transactions. With all this complexity, what's a senior manager or board member to do? Should rocket scientists run financial institutions? Should a PhD be a requirement of all senior executives and board members?

In the old days, individuals were appointed to boards or to senior management positions because of their extensive experience, which often meant a good combination of knowledge and gut-feel instincts acquired over the years. Since the availability of information was limited, this experience-based gut feel played a significant role in applying sound human judgment in decision making. Over the years, as the availability of information has become almost infinite, a good part of the gut-feel instinct to assess the situation has been replaced by numbers and models. While such information has improved the quality of variables that go into decision making, almost all significant decisions still require sound human judgment, which remains dependent upon experience and wisdom.

"If it seems too good to be true, then it probably is" used to be the old mantra. Now, something too good to be true is often mistakenly assumed to be a result of super-intelligent, complex quant analyses. Despite all the complexities, shouldn't sound human judgment have said something about AIGFP raking in so much money that they almost didn't know what to do with it?

How does one reconcile wisdom with the complexities of today's financial industry revenue model?

Board members and senior executives are not expected to know and comprehend all the complexities. They are not expected to stay a step ahead of the PhDs in terms of all the technical analyses. But they *are* expected to apply wisdom that guides them to ask critical and relevant questions to get a handle on what is critical for the company. Probing and understanding why AIGFP was raking in so much money didn't require an intimate knowledge of complex equations and the rocket science employed.

At Boeing, board members and senior executives are not expected to know the complex intricacies that can cause lithium-ion batteries to burn and explode in a Dreamliner. But they *are* expected to ask relevant questions to bring attention to critical strategic and operating issues to push the company to manage and deal with this problem satisfactorily.

When Lou Gerstner became the CEO of IBM after his years at American Express, what did he know about the huge company and its computer hardware manufacturing business? Yet he successfully ran IBM and transformed it into a stronger company during his years at the helm.

Financial institutions' senior management and board members are not expected to have read all 850 pages of the Dodd-Frank bill and comprehend it. But they are expected to obtain adequate information from the company and other reliable sources to understand what the implications are for their institutions.

Sophisticated quantitative analyses, with all the complex algorithms, equations, and formulas, only supplement the gut feel and do not provide all the answers and nuances that are required to exercise sound judgment. Despite the use of such sophisticated tools to improve the quality of information, how sound human judgment is arrived at has not changed over the years.

Asking the right questions and having the capability to comprehend critical information about the revenue models and all the associated risks is perhaps the most fundamental requirement at the senior level. Individuals in these positions need to probe and understand the company's major lines of business, how these businesses make money, what marketplace risks and challenges they face, how they are being managed, etc. This includes understanding what tools are used, how they are used, and what their limitations are in relation to the management of critical variables that drive revenue models and risks.

Board members depend upon the information fed to them by the company. However, an excuse that the information wasn't provided or was too complex should never be acceptable. Even setting up an independent parallel reporting system for the board, which is not advocated here at all, would not address the complexity or adequacy question if board members don't know and ask for the crucial information they need.

So my first key point is that senior executives and board members must develop an understanding of critical issues—related to both upside as well as downside—to exercise sound judgment, which was missing not just at AIG but at just about every counterparty institution.

16.4. READINESS AT THE SENIOR-MOST LEVEL

Imagine being in the middle of a 2008-like financial crisis, with all the complexities thrown at you as the financial world moves past at what may seem like supersonic speed, and having a proven CEO who is asking all the right questions, but doesn't have the knowledge of the business and its complexities. Very few such CEOs, if any, may have a fair chance of surviving such a situation.

Senior executives should probe and acquire knowledge to develop a critical understanding of the business. However, a new CEO unfamiliar with the industry or its complexities, and facing an immediate extreme financial crisis, doesn't have the luxury of asking the right questions to become an effective captain over time. Lou Gerstner had time to understand IBM. Imagine if he had to make a critical life-or-death decision about a major division under crisis on his first day as the CEO!

In a crisis, it is critical to have senior managers who understand and know the business and its complexities well. In addition to having an experienced captain at the helm, the entire team must be experienced in knowing the complexities, but—having worked together—they must also be on the same page to be effective.

There was a question of whether Martin Sullivan had the experience and bandwidth to have his arms around a highly complex business in normal times. The recognition of a huge loss along with the write-down of the portfolio by stunning amounts and the turmoil in the marketplace constituted a major crisis in June 2008. Under this scenario, appointing an untested CEO (Willumstad) with unproven capability to deal with complex financial businesses may have been like a coastal town installing a new mayor whose life-long experience as a mayor is from a desert town when a hurricane is about to make a landfall. Precious time and attention that should be used to prepare and brace for the storm would be wasted.

So my second key point is that an institution needs to have senior managers ready with proven capabilities to deal with complex institutions and as an effective team well before the crisis.

16.5. SIMPLICITY TO COUNTER COMPLEXITIES AND MAINTAIN CONTROL

In the context of the two key points outlined previously, simplicity is absolutely essential in dealing with complexities.

Imagine if managing a nuclear reactor required, in order to figure out if the core is headed towards a crisis, taking time to analyze complex equations or to understand what the calculations mean. While managing a reactor does require understanding all the complexities of equations and calculations, the managers monitoring the reactor must have something as simple as a gauge indicating *on a continuous basis* the "good/no-good" status. And a no-good status should trigger all kinds of alarms and predesigned steps to deal with the upcoming crisis.

Should alarm bells have gone off at AIG and also at counterparty institutions when exposure from tail risk crossed a threshold? The answer is an obvious yes.

Actually, such a threshold was crossed long before June 2008. During the period leading up to June 2008, all kinds of information—including sophisticated analyses—were available at AIG, but the lack of a simple, objective way to understand and keep track of exposure from tail risk may have led to the institution's inability to appreciate the seriousness of the situation. The institution continued its reliance on various complex models that are highly inadequate in relation to extreme tail risk and may even have kept institutions from taking any counteractions. Not being able to respond to the buildup of the crisis resulted in the loss of control of the situation.

So my third key point is that complexity requires simple measures to convey critical signals about exposure from extreme tail risk or anything else that can do serious damage.

16.6. CONCLUSIONS

It is great to have all the power of models and rocket science available to leverage into a competitive advantage in the marketplace. However, at the end of the day it is critical for senior managers and board members to know what the situation is in simple and plain terms.

If these three key points are not a part of an institution's list of preparing for the next extreme financial crisis, then the institution may end up with the most sophisticated analytics, but no ability to make sound decisions.

It will be like what Oscar Wilde said over a century ago: *"These people know the price of everything and the value of nothing."*

So how do you effectively deal with the ever-present threat of tail risk in a financial institution's revenue model?

> Sophisticated models are valuable in enhancing inputs for decision making, but in dealing with an extreme financial crisis, there is no substitute for sound human judgment, readiness, and simplicity to counter the complexity of today's financial institutions.

CHAPTER 17

From the Bane of the Revenue Model to a Competitive Advantage

Contents

> Tail risk can be managed to enhance an institution's survival in an extreme financial crisis and gain competitive advantage through superior sustainability management.

17.1. THE BANE OF A FINANCIAL INSTITUTION'S REVENUE MODEL

Extreme tail risk is a scary thing. It's always there, lurking around, and it can destroy financial institutions if they happen to find themselves on the wrong side in a crisis. That's why it's the bane of a financial institution's revenue model. However, handled methodically and in a disciplined way, it can be tamed into a competitive advantage.

Very few institutions who know they have a problem with tail risk decide to not do anything about it. For the institutions that ignore it, there is an expression for this. It's called "betting the farm." Institutions in such a situation hope and pray they are on the right side of the bet.

More often, institutions do not know they have a problem with tail risk until, to their surprise, they run into a crisis. The surprise element that

Managing Extreme Financial Risk

catches them off guard always works against them. Because they don't know what's coming—"How bad can it get?"—they have no control over the events that can be so devastating. Even if the institution survives, the price paid is huge – both in terms of the cost of actions taken by the institution to fight the crisis and the loss of shareholder value. However, being prepared for it—with actions that cost almost nothing in comparison to the cost of being caught off guard on the wrong side in a crisis—can make a huge difference.

In the early days of my career, I worked for a small financial institution that did very well as it rode up an economic cycle. However, when the cycle turned, it was caught completely off guard and went from being the top of the league to having the bottom fall out. It survived the immediate crisis, but never recovered from the blow. It ended up being absorbed into a larger institution a few years later, and shareholders paid a huge price for it.

17.2. URGENT NEED FOR PROACTIVE TAIL-RISK OR SUSTAINABILITY MANAGEMENT

Financial institutions have large exposure from tail risk. And over the years, it has increased very significantly for the following reason.

The financial institution revenue model has always been about how uncertainty is leveraged to earn profits. In pre-quant days, businesses were managed conservatively as expected loss values could not be quantified precisely. Anything that seemed riskier than the qualitative and subjective gut-feel comfort level was shunned.

Today, leveraging an enormous amount of historical data, expected loss values can be defined much more precisely through the use of quant models. Therefore, risk that may have been avoided previously can now be assumed if it is priced right. As a result, total risk has increased many-fold as indicated by the revenue growth of the last 20 years.

As discussed previously, risk arises from two components of uncertainty. With the advancement of risk management, the ability to manage risk from *quantifiable* uncertainty has improved drastically. However, during the same period, the ability to quantify and thus manage risk from *unquantifiable* uncertainty, or tail risk, has more or less stayed the same. This means that, while risk from quantifiable uncertainty has been covered by revenues (assuming sound pricing models), risk from unquantifiable uncertainty has not. As a result, the need for effective management of tail risk has increased very significantly.

17.3. PROACTIVE TAIL-RISK MANAGEMENT ENHANCES THE ABILITY TO RESPOND TO CRISES

Tail risk is an inherent part of a financial institution's revenue model. The real issue is how large is too large and how to manage it. The first thing that can make a difference is to avoid being caught off-guard. That means knowing continuously where things stand in relation to exposure from tail risk. This enables preplanned actions that maintain control, rather than responding with reactions when there is very little control.

As discussed earlier, a financial institution model is based upon marketplace confidence. For this reason two factors make a critical difference in a financial crisis. Having a cushion of liquidity buys time, and having time is a big advantage in a crisis. However, liquidity alone will not save an institution if its going-concern status is in question. Therefore, preplanned actions taken proactively will have a far greater punch than actions taken reactively. Secondly, if communicated properly through continuous dialoging with the marketplace, being ready with proactive actions can keep a crisis of confidence from materializing in the first place.

17.4. EFFECTIVE SUSTAINABILITY MANAGEMENT LEADS TO MANY SIGNIFICANT ADVANTAGES

17.4.1. Advantage: Greater Confidence in Risk Management

Despite the more precise quantification of expected loss values and the use of sophisticated models, one is always looking over one's shoulder while managing risk today to avoid being caught off guard due to the risk from unquantifiable uncertainty.

While risk management continues to drive the revenue engine, effective sustainability management enables continuous monitoring and proactive readiness to deal with the exposure from extreme tail risk that arises from unquantifiable uncertainty. Therefore, within sound risk management parameters, an institution can leverage sustainability management to run its business with greater confidence than if it needed to constantly look over its shoulder for exposure from tail risk. This translates into a direct competitive advantage in the marketplace.

17.4.2. Advantage: Readiness to Capture Marketplace Opportunities

Effective sustainability management translates into readiness in crises. Being ready and having a continuous handle on the exposure from tail risk enables an institution to take advantage of marketplace opportunities, particularly when there may be turmoil in the market. Two of the three examples summarized in Chapter 9 show that one organization profited from an extreme crisis because it was prepared, while another was paralyzed and had to sweat out many anxious days in another extreme crisis because it was highly unprepared.

This readiness also translates into a significant advantage for the financial system, as in any financial crisis markets are better off with more buyers than less. Players whose focus remains on market opportunities because they are prepared continue to be active and thus provide the much-needed market liquidity in a distressed environment, whereas those caught off guard need to focus on fighting a crisis rather than being active in the market.

Therefore, readiness derived from effective sustainability management leads to a competitive advantage in the marketplace.

17.4.3. Advantage: Reduced Regulatory Risk

As discussed in Chapter 14, a focus on sustainability leads to the convergence of the interests of the institution and the objectives of regulators. Aligned interests always turn hostilities into parties working towards common goals, thus reducing regulatory risk at the institution. This advances an institution's wellbeing.

17.4.4. Advantage: Enhanced Shareholder Value

The market value of an investment is a function of the future cash flow, discounted for the time value and the risk perceived. Effective sustainability management helps in two ways. One, it increases the quality of earnings from the advantages listed previously. Two, because of effective ongoing communications with the marketplace as outlined in Chapter 15, it reduces investor anxiety. Both factors reduce the perception of risk among investors, and thus decrease the discounting of the projected future cash flow. This enhances shareholder value.

> Effective sustainability management not only makes exposure from tail risk manageable and enhances an institution's going-concern integrity, it also translates into key advantages in the marketplace.

CHAPTER 18

Adapting Organizations to Effective Sustainability Management

Contents

> The question for boards of directors is not whether to adopt sustainability management—it is how to direct their institutions to adapt to it.

Sustainability management, with a distinct objective, provides a different perspective on an institution's business. It's more than numbers and statements. In Chapter 14, an outline identifies what would constitute effective sustainability management in a financial institution. Effective sustainability management touches and impacts everything in an institution. So where should an organization begin its implementation?

18.1. ORGANIZATION FOCUS

Adapting an institution to a new discipline requires organization focus. Organization focus is not setting up boxes and titles on a chart and staffing them with personnel; that actually constitutes a part of its implementation. Organization focus is establishing an institution's priorities in such a way that they help the senior management plan and execute an implementation roadmap to achieve the objective effectively. How should an institution create the needed organization focus for sustainability management? What is the starting roadmap?

In implementing sustainability management, establishing and maintaining the correct hierarchical relationship between parameters is critical. This relationship, described in Chapter 10, is summarized again in Figure 18.1. As discussed in Chapter 10, sustainability is so fundamental that all other objectives, goals, and parameters must be addressed in the context of maintaining a going concern. Therefore, the hierarchical order as shown in Figure 18.1 must be observed to have meaningful, clear, and objective goals and targets.

Figure 18.1

In order to establish organization focus in the context of this hierarchical relationship, some critical questions need to be addressed upfront.

18.1.1. Who Should Drive Sustainability Parameters?

While the institution's entire board needs to be involved in adopting and establishing the sustainability objective and goals, it is critical to ask who should drive this objective and the accompanying goals and policies at the board level. This may sound like a simple question. However, it involves nuances that may have significant implications for ensuring that the sustainability of the institution is addressed objectively and fully, and thus it requires the board's attention.

There are tradeoffs between sustainability goals and financial goals. However, once established, there is no choice between driving financial goals that, in turn, address the traditional revenue-driving dimension of risk and driving sustainability goals that address the sustainability-related dimension of risk.

Both must be emphasized and managed simultaneously and distinctly. The need to maintain an emphasis on sustainability goals distinctly is so strong that it needs to have a driving focus independent of financial or earnings goals. Therefore, the critical question for the board of an institution is, who should drive the sustainability management parameters at the board level? Should it be the CEO who is the primary driver of financial goals and risk-management parameters? If so, then how do you ensure a distinct emphasis? Should it be a special committee of the board with the capability to deal with significant risk governance issues? Or, should it be the chairman who must be capable of grasping and driving sustainability management parameters proactively?

Each board needs to address this question, weighing all options along with their pros and cons. Such deliberations constitute the starting point for developing the organization focus for effective sustainability management and bringing about a fundamental change to enhance the ability to survive extreme crises.

18.1.2. What Should Parameters Focus on?

No dialog can begin or take place in a vacuum; it needs an appropriate context. Therefore, before the dialog about objectives and goals begins, there must be an understanding of the structure that causes the need for the sustainability objective and goals in the first place. This requires a way to quantify and express the extreme tail-risk structure. As emphasized early on in this book, to date there is no objective, transparent, and simple measure to quantify exposure from extreme tail risk. This book has offered PML and demonstrated its power as an effective quantitative measure of extreme risk.

Therefore, the PML of the institution—along the lines of the examples discussed previously—needs to be developed to provide the context for the dialog to establish sustainability-management parameters. This includes knowing the total magnitude of PML and fully understanding what makes up PML and how different businesses impact PML in different ways.

Understanding PML and its components is the second key step in adapting an organization to effective sustainability management, as it helps identify what constitutes the exposure from extreme tail risk and thus what should be addressed.

18.1.3. How Should Parameters Be Established?

Having gained a good understanding of the institution's PML and its components, the next step is to establish sustainability parameters. This starts with a discussion of what should be the sustainability objective of the institution and should involve the entire board of directors.

Establishing parameters means defining boundaries and guidelines, which are determined by goals. Since there is a trade-off between financial goals and sustainability goals, it is essential to understand this relationship so that corporate goals maximize the financial potential of the institution's business model while ensuring protection against extreme tail risk. Discussions of this trade-off will lead to goals that can drive the sustainability-management process of the institution.

Sustainability goals help drive the boundaries and policies, or parameters, which requires addressing sustainability-management issues, such as:

- What size and scope of extreme exposure parameters are acceptable?
- What will be the impact of sustainability-management goals?
- What adjustments are needed to ensure compliance with these goals?
- How much protection should be provided?
- What guidelines should drive programs to protect against extreme tail risk?
- What criteria should be used to establish an extreme exposure limit for each business segment? And, what should be the limits for each business segment?

Such issues require significant quantitative financial analyses, and addressing them will lead to an implementation roadmap for the institution.

18.2. IMPLEMENTATION

Having established the parameters, an implementation plan needs to be developed that (i) designs and creates strategies and policies to optimize cost-benefit trade-offs in managing PML and sustainability gaps within the established parameters and (ii) ensures compliance and control mechanisms. While a distinct focus is needed, the sustainability-management process can't exist as an island. It impacts financial- and risk-management functions of the institution. Therefore, bridges must be developed between sustainability parameters and other operating guidelines for the institution.

18.2.1. Incremental, not Replacement

Chapter 3 discussed the objectives of risk management, capital management, and sustainability management to emphasize that each of these disciplines serves a critical role in an institution. Sustainability management should not be perceived as replacing or competing with something that is currently done in the institution. It represents an incremental value-added managerial process that is a distinct and important part of 1 at a financial institution.

18.2.2. Evolutionary Implementation, not Revolu Imposition

The key steps outlined previously require a significant amount of financial analysis to arrive at important decisions. Therefore, sustainability management can and should begin as an initiative under the auspices of the chief financial officer rather than first establishing a new organization structure, which should evolve as the implementation progresses. On the one hand, its implementation needs to be sensitive to minimize disruption and confusion. On the other hand, its integration into the overall management process of the firm is needed for the institution to view tail risk distinctly and manage it effectively.

18.2.3. Three Effectiveness Drivers

18.2.3.1. Captain and Quarterback

Most organizations know that if it is important, it needs to have an owner, a "captain" or a "quarterback" to provide the organizational leadership. For example, for effective financial management there is a chief financial officer, for effective risk management there is a chief risk officer, and for effective information management there is a chief information officer. Similarly, if there is something that—if not managed effectively—has the potential to adversely impact a going concern, then the institution needs to view it as not only important but also critical. Therefore, a chief sustainability officer is the obvious role, not as a bureaucratic position, but to provide leadership with a critical focus. This does not mean that hiring a chief sustainability officer is the first step at an institution. As mentioned previously, the first step is defining and establishing the need, which should drive the adoption of sustainability management as a critical priority, and the steps outlined earlier should dictate when a quarterback should be designated.

18.2.3.2. Culture

While experts have studied the importance of culture extensively, it is still hard to define it in plain language and in tangible terms. Culture relates to expectations that drive individual behavior, and collective individual behavior impacts the culture. That's why values and expectations must be first defined so that the expected behavior is clear.

Objectives, goals, and policies can be developed relatively quickly, but building and establishing a new culture takes time. Effective sustainability management does not get established by simply writing objectives, goals, and policies or by issuing an edict.

In order for something as critical as sustainability management to become a part of an organization's culture, it needs to be adopted into the managerial process. This requires, among other things, training and educating managers to think differently and use the 3-D view of the risk–return equation. They must understand that sustainability-management and risk-management policies need to work in partnership; there is no conflict between them.

Actually, in this area, financial institutions have very significant experience. About 25 years ago, risk management was only a concept. Today it is an integral component of what financial institutions do. The evolution of risk management into its current role can be an excellent model for adapting organizations to sustainability management.

Organizational culture will impact how sustainability-management readiness is developed and implemented, and—as stated in Chapter 17—readiness has a direct impact on competitive advantage. Therefore, organizational cultural issues play an important role in capturing this competitive advantage.

18.2.3.3. Flexibility

While clearly defined policies are necessary to provide direction to large organizations, flexibility to adapt them to fit how the business is run is the key to effective implementation. Objectives, goals, policies, and limits should be firmly defined, but the tactical implementation needs flexibility. Just as, at the tactical level, BCP requirements for a fast-paced trading desk are different from those for credit card operations, sustainability-management programs need to make the distinction too. Otherwise they risk becoming bureaucratic exercises without necessarily achieving objectives effectively.

Flexibility is perhaps the most important of the three items discussed here. During a crisis, among what matters the most is the institution's ability to adapt itself to do what is needed to sustain the going-concern, and then take advantage of the opportunities presented by the crisis. Adapting comes easily when flexibility is part of the planning for the crisis. Therefore, it is important that the implementation of sustainability management is strategically principled and tactically flexible to capitalize on the competitive advantage derived from continuous readiness.

A quarterback, organization culture, and flexibility are th items for effective sustainability-management (or for that matter, management) implementation at a financial institution. However, without the effective deployment of key practices discussed earlier in this book—such as the definition of sound measures, quantification of tail risk, formulation of policies, and development of programs to protect capital—the three key items mentioned in this chapter are irrelevant. Equally important, without a quarterback, organization culture and the flexibility measures, quantification, policies, and programs can't be very effective either.

A board must address extreme tail risk proactively for existential reasons, or the institution will risk being vulnerable in another crisis. As shown in this book, tail risk requires an approach different from traditional risk management, and in order to ensure a going concern there is no substitute for sustainability management. Therefore, the need for sustainability management is not optional; it is a given. However, by proactively establishing the objective and goals, and driving sustainability parameters, a board can direct the institution to adapt effectively and thus bring about a fundamental change to protect itself from extreme tail risk.

18.3. CONCLUSION

The crisis of 2008 changed the financial industry's landscape. Similar to the survival process under the laws of nature, crises weed out weak institutions that cannot adapt under the laws of economics. The last crisis was only the beginning of a new marketplace ecological cycle. Companies vanishing in 2008 were the immediate victims of the weeding-out process in this cycle, and more companies will fall victim as the cycle proceeds. Institutions that adapt to deal with extreme tail risk have the best chance of surviving and thriving.

Survival as a going concern is paramount to all organizations. Institutions and regulators will find that there is no substitute for effective sustainability management. It adds significant value to institutions by enhancing quality of earnings and creating competitive advantages, while also helping to strengthen the financial system.

Effective sustainability management does not add revenues or increase profitability as measured in quarterly earnings, but it does enhance an institution's flexibility and ability to survive the exogenous factors of the marketplace in a crisis and live to fight another day. Thinking of sustainability

;ous ecological terms should remind institutions of a
Herbert Spencer[1] who coined the expression "survival
150 years ago: *"It is not the strongest of the species that
:elligent that survives. It is the one that is the most adaptable to*

Tail risk is the bane of a financial institution's revenue model, and it can lead to a destructive blow in a financial crisis if the institution is caught off guard. Going-concern sustainability management is critical in order to ensure effective management of tail risk to survive an extreme financial crisis and build a stronger financial system.

[1] British philosopher, sociologist and political theorist coined the expression "survival of the fittest" in his 1864 book *Principles of Biology* to draw parallels between his economic theories and Charles Darwin's natural selection theory in *On the Origin of Species*.

As it turned out, the bank did not have a business continuity plan for the foreign exchange trading desk at the time of the London terrorist attack in 2005. However, thanks to quick thinking by Stewart, the bank realized no major negative impact from leaving the London trading desk unattended, as all net positions were managed from the Paris and New York desks without any significant problems. Had he not given this direction, the operational interruption at the trading desk's location—with the marketplace in turmoil— would have cost the bank millions of pounds. This was a wake-up call.

Realizing how close it came to a disaster, the bank overhauled its entire operational risk-management focus following the experience of 7/7. As a result of the realization, the bank has made operational risk management a strategic priority. Today the bank is in a much better position to proactively manage an operational crisis as credible, elaborate, and realistic BCPs have been developed and implemented for all critical functions of the bank.

On July 7, 2005, life was anything but normal in London, and Mabel's Tavern seemed to be right at the center of all the mayhem. King's Cross St. Pancras, where the first bomb exploded, is only a couple of blocks to the east. Tavistock Square, the site of the bus bombing, is a couple of blocks to the southwest. The third bomb exploded almost directly deep under Mabel's Tavern on a Piccadilly Underground train just as it had left King's Cross St. Pancras towards its next stop, Russell Square, at the southern end of Marchmont Street. Public transportation didn't resume partial service on many routes until late afternoon. The Piccadilly line didn't restore full service until August 4.

Rupert and Ian didn't meet for their lunch date, as Ian's focus shifted to getting to Heathrow and catching his BA flight back to Dublin. Heathrow continued its operations without interruption. However, because of service disruptions on the Piccadilly line and total chaos in Central London, Ian couldn't find a way to get to Heathrow in time to catch his flight. He had dinner and a few pints with Rupert, but not at Mabel's Tavern, and caught a Saturday afternoon flight to Dublin. He was with his wife when she gave birth to their daughter Alana on Sunday.

Rupert closed his foreign exchange positions the following Wednesday and netted a profit of £3,732,000 for the bank.

The Wall Street Journal
March 19, 2013

THE FED'S STRESS TESTS ADD RISK TO THE FINANCIAL SYSTEM

Banks have a powerful incentive to get the results the Fed wants and ignore other potential dangers.

By TIL SCHUERMANN

On March 14, after the markets closed, the 29 banks that hold about three-fourths of U.S. banking assets waited to hear if they passed or failed the Federal Reserve's annual stress tests. The results seemed reassuring. The Fed gave a passing grade to 14 and a failing grade to two, required two others to address some additional weakness by later this year, and didn't disclose its conclusions about the 11 smaller institutions.

Stress-testing got us out of the financial crisis in May 2009, and it has since become the crisis-management tool of choice in the banking industry. But how well is it serving the country?

One unquestionably positive result is that banks have built up the capabilities to see how they would fare through different crisis scenarios. They must consider a mind-bending array of outcomes and have enough capital to deal with them—from what might happen to checking accounts and mortgages, to all those loans to develop shopping malls, to the derivatives that grease the global financial system. Bank regulators now can develop their own views of those questions and, more important, of the answers given by the banks.

This is a sea change. Regulators are always at an informational disadvantage—they don't underwrite loans or structure derivatives, they just try to check up on them. Before 2009, the only advantage a regulator had was the ability to see across all banks, comparing the answers and methodologies for reaching them. But there is no substitute for building your own models and coming to your own view. That is what the 2009 stress test did.

Since that first stress test, the financial ecosystem has seen an explosion of statistical and economic modeling. This is a positive development. I've done economic and financial modeling for two decades, including designing the Fed's quantitative assessment architecture for stress testing, which is the basis for the central bank's current process (the Comprehensive Capital Analysis and Review). Stress-testing has led to innovative thinking about risk assessment.

But there is another side to this. As the Fed's models have become more and more important in deciding the fate of the biggest banks, those banks have focused more and more on trying to mimic the Fed's results rather than tracing out their own risk profiles. This poses a real risk.

Remember that in late 2008 the largest U.S. bank holding companies were all adequately capitalized by regulatory standards. The market had a different view: Most were trading at less than book value.

It was only by trying something new, and by disclosing enough details so the market could "check the math," that bank regulators were able to regain the confidence of the public, and for the public to regain confidence in the banking system. Yet this "something new"—the formal stress-testing so important for the guardians of the financial system—is now inhibiting innovation among those that need guarding.

The incentives to get close to the Fed's numbers are powerful enough to stifle genuine creativity, imagination and innovation by risk managers and their modelers. Deviating from standard industry practice is now increasingly viewed with suspicion and often discouraged by bank regulators.

I understand this suspicion from my own days at the Fed: The modeling machinery built for the first stress test was in no small part designed to have an independent view on the output of "innovative" but dangerously flawed bank risk models, such as those for mortgage losses. But if everybody uses the same scenario (which they do) and works hard to get the same numbers (and they are trying), then we have a very narrowly specialized risk machine that is inflexible and unresponsive to unexpected shocks. That is, shocks that weren't previously subject to a stress-test.

The danger is that the financial system and its regulators are moving to a narrow risk-model gene pool that is highly vulnerable to the next financial virus. By discouraging innovation in risk models, we risk sowing the seeds of our next systemic crisis.

Mr. Schuermann, a former senior vice president at the Federal Reserve Bank of New York, is a partner at Oliver Wyman's financial services practice.

INDEX

Note: Page numbers with "*f*" denote figures; "*t*" tables; and "*b*" boxes.